D0021199

IMMELMANN
"The Eagle of Lille"

IMMELMANN
"The Eagle of Lille"

By
FRANZ IMMELMANN
Translated from the German by Claud W. Sykes

With
THE VICTORIES OF MAX IMMELMANN
An Appendix by Norman L. Franks

CASEMATE
Philadelphia & Newbury
A Greenhill Book

This edition of *Immelmann: The Eagle of Lille* is published in
the United States of America in 2009 by
CASEMATE
1016 Warrior Road, Drexel Hill, PA 19026

and in the United Kingdom by
CASEMATE
17 Cheap Street, Newbury, RG14 5DD

 *A Greenhill Book*

Copyright © 1990 & 2009 Lionel Leventhal Ltd

Appendix © Norman L. Franks 1990

Typeset & design © Casemate Publishers 2009

ISBN 978-1-932033-98-4

Cataloging in publication data is available from the
Library of Congress and the British Library.

Printed and bound in the United States of America

Publishing History:
Immelmann, The Eagle of Lille was first published in German as *der Adler von Lille*
by K.F. Koehler Verlag, Leipzig in 1934. The first English edition was published by
John Hamilton in 1935 or 1936. It was reissued in facsmile by Greenhill Books /
Lionel Leventhal Ltd in 1990 with a new appendix by Norman Franks. This new edi-
tion has been completely retypeset but the original language has been left unaltered.

Contents

Introduction

When we airmen climbed out of our cockpits after our final front patrols in the gloomy days of November, 1918, only very few of us realised that those were the last flights we should ever make; also that for long, long years the Treaty of Versailles would leave us nothing but memories and longings. The longing for the vast expanse of the air was destined to become almost a torture to us at times when we gazed at the blue sky and watched one of the few German airmen careering in and out of some particularly beautiful cumulus cloud.

Then, in the hard struggle for existence, our longings were lulled to sleep.

Our ancient longing for the air is awake once more. And so—impelled by this longing—for some time past I have been looking through the souvenirs left to me from the days of my Great War experiences. Quite unexpectedly I put my hands on a packet of letters—the letters written by my brother Max to our mother during the war.

I dip into them, and suddenly a vision rises up of the glorious days when we could fly and when—since we were war airmen—we could gain our own experience of the war which, despite Staffel and Squadron patrols revealed itself to us only in the way in which my brother Max saw it in his first combat patrols... as a knightly duel between two evenly matched opponents. Was it the war we loved, or the flying?

In my opinion it was the flying. Whence, else, comes that last vestige of longing we feel today when we hear a propeller humming in the blue of heaven?

Faded press cuttings recall those days and our common experiences in them. Yes, it was a happy, youthful, vigorous life we led then, and it brought my brother Max to the highest military fame and to the greatest and most genuine popularity. And was he not fortunate also in his end, since Providence summoned him away from this earth at the height of his popularity, when he was still the unconquered ruler of his airy domain and the Eagle of Lille? That name was given to him in esteem and admiration by his opponents in the trenches on the other side of the line.

He was likewise fortunate in that he was spared witnessing the bitter end. He remained ever a true believer in the German ideals, and it was fortunate for him that he was not forced to experience the unworthy and unnecessary self-abasement of those men of November, 1918, the odious self-mutilation of his compatriots and the inexpressibly wearisome fourteen years of Germany's decline.

I think on the days of youth which we shared. Then I rummage in mother's desk and find some carefully guarded treasures there—the youthful letters of her eldest son—childhood's memories—souvenirs....

And it is not merely the kindred nature which now takes such strong possession of me and reveals my better self to me. No, it is the fact that something which has been buried now emerges to my view. I see the portrait of a true German, who was unrestrainedly proud of being a German.

But at the same time I realise with some amazement what

a tender core there was in the depths of this self-controlled nature. He was tender in his love of home and country and touching in his devotion to our mother. Full of melancholy, I read the bitterest self-reproaches made by the seventeen-year-old cadet because his firm resolve to leave the cadet corps troubled his beloved mother ... and then the later letters of the ensign depicting the happiness he would experience when he could live with her again ... and last, the airman, always endeavouring by means of long descriptions to give mother at least some share in all his beautiful experiences. And so we may understand how irreplaceable her eldest son was to the mother, how the memories of him lived on in her and how inconsolable she is because the German nation appears to have forgotten him for the moment.

But Germany is again 'a nation of airmen'; she must and shall not forget the man who rightly called himself an enthusiastic airman and was one of the early pioneers of Germany's deeds in the air.

And if the publication of his letters, the sketch of his life which I have drawn from my fraternal experiences, and the attempt to give an appreciation of his achievements in the air which I have made should succeed in keeping the memories of him alive, then the true purpose of this book is as follows:

To set to our youth of today, which stands for our future airmen and our hopes for the future, an example which shall show them that they cannot achieve true greatness by virtue of any presumptive rights but only by loyalty in small things as well as great, together with idealism, unquestioning fulfilment of duty in the sphere in which each one has his place for the common good and the subordination of the individual self which was practised by our constellation of three shining stars: *Immelmann, Boelcke, Richthofen.*

I

Early Days

CHILDHOOD

If man is said to be the product of his education, it is with this limitation, that even the best education cannot make up for defective qualities. Our qualities are immutable gifts from our ancestors, which have been deposited with us in our cradles, and it is the task of education to develop these qualities.

If we judge Max Immelmann, who was born on September 21st, 1890, at Dresden, from this standpoint, we find him endowed with the preliminary conditions for a successful career. From his father, Franz Immelmann, who owned and managed a cardboard factory, he inherited the tenacity, thoroughness and perseverance of the Uckermark ancestors who struck such deep roots in their native soil and from his mother, the daughter of Chief Auditor Grimm, the sense of duty, self-control and steadfastness of purpose that came from the blood of generations of government officials.

When bereaved of her husband after a short marriage, the mother sought support from her eldest son when he was still young, and found such measure of it as a mother seldom finds from any son. No easy task lay before mother and son, and they did not seek to make it easy. The mother had to educate her three children, and did so, while Max soon recognised that it was his mission to support his mother and set an example to his brother and sister.

For the first eight years of her marriage the mother had to fight, almost without outside assistance, against the ravages of illness. She did not possess a strong constitution, and not only was she forced to bring Max safely through some obstinate childish complaints in his first three years, but

Franz, her second son, was at death's door, and the doctors gave up hope of his recovery. When the two boys were over the worst, their little sister fell ill and had to undergo a throat operation, in the course of which she nearly bled to death.

In the midst of all these troubles and anxieties on behalf of her children, the mother had to nurse her husband, who was ill for four years. As the doctors were unable to give her ailing family any real help, she soon looked round for new methods and turned to natural therapeutics. After first testing everything on herself, she tided her children over the critical months. Max grew into a sturdy little fellow who radiated strength; Franz, the candidate for Death's realm, became a huge, fiery chap, while the little sister was a lively, obstinate doll of a girl. But all three had a firm hold on life when their father died in 1897.

Our mother's experiences with the Nature treatment for her children in their early years were signposts for their further upbringing. Constantly keeping her eyes open for modern methods and taking note of all progress in the world from which she could extract benefit, she sought to educate her children in the new spirit. She nourished their bodies on a simple vegetarian diet and hardened them by physical exercise and courses of training.

Max also grew into a meditative little fellow who, even in his earliest years, could follow a train of thought to most amazing deductions after long and careful consideration. Thus, when he was five years old, his Aunt Boetzel told him that the world was as round as a ball, but much larger. Some while afterwards she found the little chap sitting quietly on the garden lawn; he passed one little finger meditatively round his ball and then said to her: "If I go out of the garden door and keep on running, I shall get back to the other side of the garden, because the world is as round as my ball."

At a very early age he showed a studious disposition and a love for anything technical. He could never find any pleasure in playing with his younger brother's soldiers and barred them from admission to the extensive railway systems which he and his friend, Otto Küster, spent many hours in building in their rooms. Never, even in his earliest childhood, did he break up toys frivolously, as so many children do. If his thirst for knowledge and his desire to see the inward mechanism of some object impelled him to take it to pieces, he always put it together again, even though it often cost him hours of tedious work.

He was true to these childish principles in his later treatment of bicycle, motor-cycle, motor-car and aero-plane. "I must have a look at it," he would say, and then he took it to pieces, for he set no account on mere book-learning, but always held fast to the results of his own investigations and practical tests. When Brother Franz acquired a motor-cycle in 1909 (an antediluvian affair; it could only be mounted by means of a ladder) it was amazing to see the skill with which Max took the engine to pieces and even more so to note the expert way in which he assembled it again. As motor-cycles were rarities in those days and Max had never handled one before, this feat was evidence of very great technical ability.

In this respect he remained unchanged to the end. He always had to see how everything was done, even in the case of his first Fokker.

"I asked Boelcke to take me up once," he wrote on August 3rd, 1915, "because I wanted to see how he handled the controls."

Books and the knowledge to be derived from them did not mean much to him. He could not understand why his brother and sister, both of whom were keen readers, devoured all the obtainable literature; he, for his part, refused to open these books. Not until considerably later did he gain some appreciation of the worth of books by his contact with popular works on physics and mathematics and finally with technical publications.

Despite the meditative nature which revealed itself at an over-early age, Max was never a spoil-sport. He took his share with all the other boys in the games of soldiers and robbers which made the 'White Stag' in the neighbourhood of Dresden an unsafe abode for the guests staying there (in fact, the latter regarded the Immelmann children as the wildest of the wild), while later he and his friend Küster were most redoubtable Indian chiefs in the Pawel woods. Acting on the wise instructions of Küster—then a member of the fifth form—he followed the latter's example in smoking the forbidden cigarettes (price one pfennig apiece; to 'improve their quality', they had to be kept in store for several months in the school desks); like all the other young ruffians residing in the Rudolfstrasse in Brunswick, he took part in the street battles waged against the gang that inhabited the Oelper-strasse. But these boyish pranks were never allowed to cause any serious anxiety to the mother who gave her children a generous measure of freedom, and the timely self-control he exercised was always a good example to his wilder brother and sister. But just because the mother never set her eldest son up as an example, his steady character, which grew firmer and firmer, exercised the best possible influence upon them.

Tussles with the fiery Franz were inevitable. Although the

latter was as strong as his elder brother, he was always vanquished in the end by the greater tenacity and persistence of the unruffled Max, who never hammered him, but merely held him down until he gave his promise to keep the peace. Franz grew to realise the futility of his excitable outbursts against his brother and developed a will to restrain his impetuosity; in this fashion Max achieved all unconsciously valuable educational work in connection with his younger brother.

SCHOOL AND CADET DAYS

Only a very few experiences of the days of our youth have remained in my memory. The reason for this may be that, viewed through the eyes of children, our mode of life did not differ greatly from that of our contemporaries. Moreover we did not see anything particularly note-worthy in the many removals occasioned by the illness of our father.

When we moved from the neighbourhood of Dresden to Brunswick in 1902, we could not understand why Max burst into a sudden fit of weeping on passing 'his' Royal Grammar School in the cab on the way to the Neustadt station. But he had taken his native town of Dresden so deeply into his small schoolboy heart that the departure was the heaviest possible blow to him, for I cannot remember having seen Max in tears on any other occasion. Like my mother, he was wishing himself back in Dresden all the time we were in Brunswick, with the result that we returned thither in 1904.

But those two years in Brunswick were certainly the most beautiful ones of our youth. Max attended the Royal Martino Katharineum Grammar School, where he made the acquaintance of Otto Küster, with whom he remained on terms of closest friendship until his death.

In the glorious, untroubled freedom of youth we two schoolboys roamed the mysterious corridors and vaults of the Boetzel family's wine cellars; in the summer we made the vast expanses of the Pawel woods unsafe for pedestrians and in the winter we made a nuisance of ourselves to the skaters on the rinks of the Civic Pond and the small parade ground.

When we were in Brunswick, we two boys paid our first visits to our grandfather, who was the district veterinary surgeon at Stendal. As nippers of ten and eleven, we went off proudly on the first journey we ever took alone and entered the town of our forefathers through its ancient gates.

When our mother returned to Dresden in 1904, my wildness caused me to be boarded out. Max—then in the fourth form of the Royal Grammar School—found a glorious youthful paradise at the 'Weinberg' in Loschwitz, a wonderful estate belonging to our maternal grandfather, but afterwards the serious side of life began for him.

On a suggestion made by Grandfather Grimm, Max was sent at Easter, 1905, to the Dresden Cadet School, where he entered the lower third form. It was certainly no easy matter for one so accustomed to freedom to adapt himself to the strict order and discipline of the cadet corps, especially as his instructor was often forced to curtail his leave by way of punishment. I have a most melancholy military scrawl from him as a souvenir of that time, but nevertheless the miniature soldier made a great impression on me, especially as Max owned a motor-cycle—a rarity for such a young fellow of those days. Thanks to his natural manner, his orderly disposition and his great love for his mother, he soon settled down in his new surroundings, for eighteen months later he was the second senior in his room.

But while his character grew continually firmer and his own particular personality was in process of formation, views and conceptions of life originating from the up-bringing given him by his mother developed within him, and showed him the serious contrast of outlook that existed between him and his comrades of the cadet corps (he found the same contrast later when he became an ensign). When he realised this difference of outlook, he was ready to draw the consequences, and in 1908 he proposed to leave the cadet corps and devote his life to some profession of a technical nature. Moved by his mother's pleading and his own love for her, he decided to stay at the school until he had passed his leaving certificate examination, but in 1912, when he was an ensign, he returned to his original intention of taking up some technical profession.

The reasons which Max adduced in that letter to his mother—written at the age of seventeen—for his resolve to leave the corps are very illuminative, for they show in their essence precisely the same standpoint as that which impelled him to renounce a military career in 1912.

In this letter of January, 1908, he informs his mother that his comrades chaffed him for his repugnance to any form of meat food and his dislike of alcohol. He says that he would like to be a soldier, but that he has no desire for an officer's career because he does not wish to be bound by the stiff etiquette of a particular caste.

Having been brought up from our early youth mainly on the principles laid down by Dr. Lachmann, we spent our long summer holidays of 1906 and 1907 in Just's nature cure establishment in the Harz Mountains, where, in Max's case, the lectures given by Just on reformed modes of life fell on particularly fruitful soil. He always remained faithful to the views which he formed at that time. Although he adapted himself to his surroundings at a riper age, he nevertheless always ate vegetarian food whenever possible and invariably refused alcohol and nicotine. Shortly before his death he gave expression in writing on his attitude towards alcohol: " ... In fact, I consider that there is nothing more paralyzing or more deteriorative than the consumption of spirits in any form. I have had personal opportunity to observe the unfavourable influence exerted by even the smallest quantities of alcohol on will-power, thought-capacity and presence of mind. I need not say anything concerning the bad effects of a debauch, because even the greatest friends of alcohol have seen clear evidence of the physical and mental harm it causes. As for every other man in control of a swift vehicle, such as a motorist or an engine-driver, so for us airmen abstention from alcohol is a basic necessity if we are to achieve success without having to complain of overstrained nerves . . ."

But in 1908 Max allowed himself to be convinced that it would be better for his future studies if he remained in the corps and took his certificate there.

During his last years in the cadet corps his personality moulded itself into the form in which it expresses itself in his war letters. He was a calm and thoughtful man, affable and modest, but self-assured and self-reliant.

One of his last school reports is a characteristic description of his disposition and development. It emphasises his decided predilection for all mathematical subjects (Chemistry Ib, Physics I, Mathematics, Geometrical Drawing Ib). His knowledge of languages was only 'sufficient' (Latin, French and English 3).

The verdict of his company commander is as follows:

By reason of his good character and qualities Immelmann has a very sympathetic nature, with excellent deportment.

Home work—praiseworthy.

He has justified his position as senior of his room and takes a lost of trouble; he looks after the younger cadets well.

In practical service he is one of the best; his bearing is definite and full of assurance.

Conduct—excellent.

Since 1908 Max had subjected his body to his own hard schooling, and I, who have never possessed the endurance powers of my elder brother, was often amazed during our youth at the obstinate patience with which Max could practise some physical exercise for hours on end. Consequently he became an excellent gymnast, and his performances as a trick cyclist and an acrobat in the cadet displays given at Christmas and on the Emperor's birthday excited more admiration every year from his superiors, his comrades and the guests.

Among my brother's pre-war letters there are some particularly charming ones which he wrote to my mother about a holiday in the Alps in 1909 with three comrades. They show a remarkable power of observation, so that their copious contents enable one to share with him all the events of the journey from Dresden to Salzburg, Berchtesgaden, Tobalch, Cortina, Innsbruck and Munich. In this fashion he gives descriptions of the wonderful show-clad Tauern peaks, an ascent of the Glockner and the overwhelming beauty of the glacier.

"Yesterday we climbed the Franz Joseph peak, 2,453

meters," he writes. "From there we saw the whole Glockner area wonderfully lit up by the sun, and to the right of it there was the snow-white Johannisberg. In the foreground one sees the shimmering, sea-green Pasterze, in the middle the sharply rising Glockner with its hut perched up 3,400 meters high and in the background the Johannisberg which forms a contrast to the Glockner by showing not a single rock. The lower part is all glacier, and on its upper part it has a cap of snow. With a dazzling sun in an almost cloudless sky the whole picture makes a most overwhelming impression. Generally I am not given to excess of enthusiasm, but all four of us sat on the grass for over an hour without uttering a word. All too soon came the moment for departure, but we found it very difficult to leave the place. I have sent you the most beautiful post cards I could find, but they are only miserable clumsy imitations of Nature."

He did all the hardest stages of the journey on foot and would not yield to the persuasion of his companions to utilise conveyances, because "by tramping and climbing one has so much more of glorious Nature and when it is over one can be glad of the money saved."

The journey lasted three weeks. From it he brought home enthusiastic impressions and a wealth of photographic material.

But in the next year (1910), Max came to us with a special plan for his last summer holiday in the cadet corps. He wanted to make a long cycle tour, and I was to accompany him for as much of it as possible. This plan was put into execution, and within a fortnight we cycled via Brussels (World Exhibition) to Paris and thence to Boppard on the Rhine, where our mother and sister spent the rest of the holidays with us.

As Max's holidays began a few days before my own, he cycled from Dresden to Cologne, where I joined him by train.

I still remember that trip. On one occasion we lay down to pass the night on the outskirts of a wood. When it began to rain later on, we rolled ourselves—still dazed with sleep—into the shelter of the trees, but woke up the next morning to find ourselves quite close to a precipice to the brink of which we had rolled.

One of the notable features of this trip was our departure for Paris with a total of three francs in our pockets and a stretch of about 400 kilometres before us. We got as far as Fère-en-Champenoise and then had to wait there for a week without a centime until money from our dear mother reached us. As from the very beginning the people of the inn where we lodged suspected us of intentions to swindle them, our bill of fare grew scantier and scantier from day to day. On another occasion we slept the night in a strawstack somewhere near Compiègne, but were roused in the early morning by the sound of French bugles. Peering cautiously out of our straw, we found ourselves in the centre of a French infantry regiment which had bivouacked there.

When I flew daily over the great Roman road from La Ville aux Bois to Rheims in 1917, I often thought of the time seven years before, when we pedalled along it in scorching heat. I wonder whether it ever recalled similar memories to Max.

At last, at Easter 1911, the 'Gate of Freedom' opened, and an annual contingent of cadets was released for the army. Max hoped for nothing from this 'freedom'. When choosing his future regiment, he had said that as an officer he would find none which could satisfy his most urgent desire for practical technical work. He hesitated for a long while between the pioneers and the railway corps, and finally applied to the latter, which accepted him.

The fact that his first firm resolve to doff his uniform and devote himself entirely to his studies was made when he was stationed with the railway experimental section at Wunsdorf-Finsterwald proves the fact that the army had no satisfactory technical occupation to offer him.

And so those glorious ensign days which are generally the best for the youngsters meant nothing for Max but a period of severe inner conflicts, and all the more so because his sense of honour and his heart could not reconcile themselves to much that he saw and experienced during his life as an ensign.

THE ENSIGN

"So allow Youth the privilege of finding its own way by groping and seeking."

When the youngest ensign of the Second Railway Regiment made his entry into the barracks at Schöneberg, near Berlin, on April 4th, 1911, no notice was taken of him, because the name Immelmann meant nothing to anyone there. All had forgotten—probably because he came from Saxony—that the regiment had accepted an Ensign Immelmann. By virtue of the regimental letter of acceptance the matter was naturally looked into, but it may have been depressing experience for the young man, who was entering upon a new phase of his life with some excitement, to have to go from one office to another as a person whose existence had been forgotten.

His service with the railwaymen was destined to prove as disappointing as his entrance. The purely military side of it, as for instance, the training of the recruits, was nothing new to a cadet N.C.O. who had been the senior of his room, but he was also forced to recognise that the technical work, on account of which he had chosen the railway corps, was limited to the application of certain definite, rigid building and working regulations, and that as far as he could see, he would have no further possibilities of progress in the kind of education he desired.

When he was serving in Wunsdorf, his efforts to acquire expert knowledge about practical work from the technicians whose co-operation had been enlisted found no understanding. Thereupon his old misgivings were awakened, and he doubted whether an officer's career was the right one for him. "How," he writes, "can they take it amiss because I respect the knowledge and the practical work of anyone, even though he is only a simple workman, and try to profit by it?"

Since his expectations were so far from fulfilment, he looked forward with pleasure to the provisional termination of his regimental service, which he had performed to the complete satisfaction of his superiors. At the beginning of August, 1911, he was posted to the War Academy at Anklam.

But there he was only confirmed in his opinion that he was unsuited to an officer's career. His first hints that he intended to change his profession naturally met with the liveliest opposition from his mother, who had been happy to see her eldest son in an assured and respected position.

"So allow Youth the privilege of finding its own way by groping and seeking," Max thereupon wrote to his mother, and truly, after long searches and investigations, which he prosecuted later in co-operatiòn with his mother, he won his way to the grave decision to ask for a transfer to the reserve as soon as he had passed his officer's examination, in order to study mechanical engineering.

His letters which deal with the battles he waged in the course of this inner conflict show that he never felt inclined to hang his head, and he never did so. "…You seem to think," he wrote from Anklam at the end of November, "that I do not feel at ease here, but that is by no means the case. I do my little job, and feel thoroughly happy."

His superiors were also satisfied with him, and he found another hobby in addition to his mathematics and acrobatic performances—a motorcycle.

The following excerpts from his letters show the contentment he found in these pursuits and the way in which he analysed the question: officer or engineer, as well as giving us an insight into the life of a War Academy of those days.

"Oct. 1911.
If I had not my Sundays and my motor cycle on Sundays, I should have been fed up here long ago. Most of the others go dancing on Sundays or in the Traube wine-restaurant or in Hille's confectionery, where I often go too.

Last Sunday was the finest I have spent here.

I swung myself on to my motor cycle at 10.30 a.m. and rode through a very wet wood to reach the Greifswald (40 kilometres from Anklam) at 11.30. I lunched there. Then I started off again at 12.30 and reached Stralsund on the dot of one after a fast run along a good stretch of road. I did the 39 kilometres in 30 minutes, that is to say, at a speed of 78 kilometres an hour. The feeling of being left entirely to oneself and a small engine when whirling along at such a pace is simply glorious. You do not feel any jerks or jolts, because they are all absorbed by the springs.

I reached the harbour about two, boarded a steamer and went across to Rügen. On the steamer I had an argument with the owner of a car, who maintained that motor cycles could not run properly. I challenged him to a race, and he agreed; we were to start as soon as we landed on the island, our goal being Bergen, which is 25 kilometres away. I was the first off the ferry and whizzed away at once; five minutes later the car caught me up. Then I gave my motor cycle some more gas, and after another ten minutes I overhauled that car in fine fashion in spite of its 40 h.p. and finished six minutes ahead. I did the stretch in 20 minutes. As soon as the car began to do 65 kilometers an hour, it wobbled and was in danger of lurching off the road. I turned back and made off homewards when I reached Bergen; the return journey passed off just as smoothly, but I had to go more slowly because of the gathering darkness.

Now I am living on this pleasure from Sunday to Wednesday. On Thursday I shall plan out another trip and enjoy the anticipation of it until Saturday. Then on Sunday comes the trip, and then the memories of it, etc.... and so the time will pass."

"*Nov. 25th.*
... A boring Sunday today. I have written out a paper on the activities of the wireless section in the battles of the Waterberg, in German South-West Africa, on August 11th, 1908. Then I did some more mathematics, just as I did last Sunday. That is the best for me.

Whenever I find any time, I read mathematical works. The study of military tactics, which are the basis of an officer's career, leave me completely cold. Tactics are mainly a matter of intuition, so that one can learn only their most general principles. I am always amazed at the way many ensigns here can say the right thing in questions of tactics at the first attempt, just as the others are amazed when anyone's motor cycle will not work and I say at the first inspection: 'This or that is wrong.'

... I find myself in a continuous state of doubt—whether to go or stay. I am constantly weighing the pros and cons. Sometimes I say to myself: 'I shall soon be through, and then I shall belong to a profession which ranks at the top of the list. But if I go, I shall have to spend several years of work in trying to procure a life-job, but then I shall have a profession which seems likely to satisfy me and which will enable me to order my mode of life in the way which you and I think the better one.

... Today the examinations come to an end. They have gone off very well for me. I got sixes for field service knowledge, map-drawing, fortification and arms knowledge, five for tactics and seven for military correspondence. You know that the marking is the same as in the cadet corps, where nine is the best and one the worst.

There is a show here on December 21st. I am going to perform as a cyclist. My inspection officer has asked me to.

I did not go out on any trip last Sunday. I worked at mathematics from ten to one in the morning and from two to ten afterwards, and got through not less than eighty exercises.

As I have seen from examples here, even the officers who attend the Military-technical Academy later on are only used as superior foremen. They know too little to be proper engineers.... Why shouldn't I study in Dresden? It would be a pity to go elsewhere, for there is no town in which I feel so happy as in Dresden.

... I am going to stop brooding now, for firstly it has no purpose, and secondly, I have finished considering the matter. I know now what I shall do."

"January 12th.
... As I wrote to you, I have gone into training a bit for the Emperor's birthday.

The dress rehearsal was on January 24th. It was open to anyone in Anklam who wanted to come and pay for entrance. The show started at 7 p.m. My turn went very well. I was quite satisfied, because they clapped me heartily. To my great dismay I saw our commander shake hands with the individual performers and thank them for their trouble, and I was the only one to whom he did not say anything.

The next morning I was suddenly summoned to the commander. I couldn't think what was the matter, and wondered whether anything in my turn had displeased him. When I reported to him, he said:

'I was looking for you all yesterday evening, but could not find you. I wanted to thank you for your trouble. I cannot express the astonishment I felt when I saw your performance, which was simply marvellous! I have served in various War Academies for a matter of twelve years, but have never seen anything approaching it. I wish you the best of luck for to-night, and you can be sure that you are easily the star turn.'

As you can imagine, I was quite consoled.

I cannot put on to paper all the things that were said to me on the night. Wherever I went, whether I was eating, drinking or dancing, I heard everyone talking about the 'marvellous acrobat'. I was introduced to the cream of society, and they all praised me. I was not introduced as

Immelmann, but as 'the acrobat'. The commander dragged me along from one to the other. Ever so often someone said to me: 'Well, if you ever get kicked out of the Army, you can get a job with Busch's circus!' If I had drained my glass for everyone who wanted to drink with me, I should have died of alcoholic poisoning!

In our classes yesterday one of the captains spoke about the show, but did not mention me when he passed judgment on the others. Then at the end he said: 'It would be presumption to criticise Immelmann. Your performance was above all criticism; I should not have thought it possible to see anyone doing such things as an amateur!"

At the end of January, 1912, the War Academy made an instructional tour to Thorn, via Stettin and Bromberg.

They visited the Grosser Kurfürst fortress, after which they went on towards the eastern frontier, where the big guns were shown and explained to them.

Finally they made the return journey via Tegel, Berlin and Johannistal, where they saw the aeroplanes. "That was the crown of our tour of instruction," he wrote. "One seldom sees anything so splendid. They showed us all the most important machines, such as the Wrights, Rumplers and Farmans, explained their construction and demonstrated three of them. It was a glorious and unique sight when these aeroplanes, which resembled huge birds, soared into the air and executed daring turns and glides with a truly amazing self-confidence."

When he returned to Anklam the old life in the lecture rooms was not resumed immediately, because he had to undergo practical courses in field-work. His term at the War Academy then came to an end with examinations, in which he obtained a 'good'. He did not send in his resignation until he knew definitely how he had done in these examinations.

"... I did not send in my resignation until yesterday," he wrote to his mother, "although it was somewhat belated. But I have my own good reasons for the delay. On March 10th there was a conference on the results of the examination, and I knew that my marks were pretty high. When the results were given, I found that my figures were 122, and the commander had said that he could be fairly safe in guaranteeing anyone with over 120. So they can't plough me just because I want to leave."

At last the War Academy term came to an end. "... So I am back with the regiment," he wrote from Berlin. "My company commander and all the other officers were most inexplicably friendly to me. Rath is really sorry that I mean to go, and he told the company officers he would have liked to keep me.

My resignation has to go the round of the offices. I don't know when it will come back."

My brother's resignation was accepted about the middle of April, and he was transferred to the reserve with the rank of swordknot ensign.

Then his wish was fulfilled, for he was able to commence his studies at the Technical High School. He was beaming with joy when he arrived in Dresden.

STUDENT DAYS

After all Max's years of schooling and the so-called 'technical service' with his regiment, he was overjoyed at the possibility of real practical work. He therefore began his studies with a sandwich course of practical work, which he took in the turbine factory at the Dresden suburb of Reick.

The joy that was his when he could find an outlet for his bear-like strength in the work he had to do with his hands must have speedily reconciled mother to his change of profession. Between her and Max there was soon established a bond of community of interests, which was as beautiful as any mother could have desired. Mother had to take her part in everything Max did. Just as she had once begun to study Latin with him, so now she was initiated into the first principles of mathematics in order that she might be able to follow technical discussions.

At that time a most remarkable kind of conveyance made its appearance in the motor market. It was an 8 h.p. motor cycle without a saddle but with a three-seater side-car. This strange 'Magnet-selfdriver' was steered by means of a wheel in the side-car.

In the winter of 1912-13 this most primitive substitute for a motor car—which incidentally cost 3,000 marks—represented the dream of Max's aspirations, but at last he acquired one. As these conveyances were manufactured in Berlin, where I was then a student, and as furthermore I was in possession of a driver's licence (which Max was not), I had the honour of bringing the 'car' to Dresden on Christmas Eve. But Max could not resist coming up to Berlin for the ceremony of taking possession.

I must divulge that it took us about sixteen hours to bring our vehicle to Dresden. We repeated the trip several times, and to the best of my recollection, our record was eleven hours. But I will not be ungrateful. This vehicle gave all of us, and expecially Max and mother, many happy hours, but above all, it enabled Max to acquire extraordinary skill in dismantling and assembling engines. After it had been in his possession for six months, however, it changed hands for a sum of 1, 500 marks, to the satisfaction of the whole family.

Since the lion had tasted blood, he naturally could not exist without a proper car. In midsummer, 1913, a real 7 h.p. Mathis filled the gaps. In spite of all its tricks there never was a car which gave so much pleasure as this Mathis.

One could not call the Mathis exactly reliable. It had to be sent home by train from all corners of Saxony, and finally it made a journey by rail from Kiel to the factory at Strassburg.

Again and again Max cheerfully took the engine to pieces, although neither the Dresden representative of the firm nor the experts in the factory had ever been able to discover what was wrong with it. With equal cheerfulness he repaired the damages I did to the car, and in the worst cases he only called me a 'greenhorn'.

And with all the work entailed by his studies and the mathematical lessons he gave in the winter of 1912 his affection let him find time to dismantle his old N.S.U motor cycle completely, overhaul it, re-enamel and re-nickel it and then put it under the Christmas tree as a present for me. How his great eyebrows screwed up with laughter that evening!

For all his devotion to cars he did not neglect other forms of sport. He joined the Academic Gymnastic Club and did a lot of gymnastics there, as well as light athletics. He danced, played tennis and skated in winter with the same keenness that he gave to his trick cycling and acrobatics. In the Reserve Officers' Association he attended lectures on military subjects and made copious contributions of his own. Thus in spite of all the great zeal and devotion he gave to his studies, his body was not allowed to deteriorate. His agility and a splendidly trained athletic physique remained intact.

Above all, he was able to live in his own way at home. Although in the opinion of our mother, who had graduated from Kneipp and Lachmann via Just to the completely rational rules of life of the Mazdaznan doctrine, he did not yet live 'rightly', and although he was no spoilsport and never refused an occasional glass of spirits, he nevertheless strengthened his robust health in this year, and with it the imperturbable serenity which he retained to the day of his death.

In addition to all these bodily activities my brother also found time to take part in an unofficial capacity in the three days Harz Mountains Winter Trials, instituted by the German Academical Automobile Club, of which he was a member, to join the Technical Aviation Association and take part in the model-building evenings for young people and finally to become a member of the Air Fleet League. I have a vision of him as an enthusiastic official darting about the old Dresden aerodrome at Caditz on the occasion of the 1913-14 triangular flight competitions.

Thus in the space of these two and a half years my brother Max acquired all the qualities which enabled him to rise within a few months from an unknown aviation pupil to one of the celebrated heroes of the air, and to lay down his life as a successful pioneer of German aviation.

II

The Outbreak of War and The Evolution of an Airman

THE OUTBREAK OF WAR

Since Max could see no prospects of satisfactory activities in peace-time service with the railway corps, the thought of spending the war with that unit must have meant even less to him.

In the times when all Germans volunteered their services with exultation, it was not a pleasant experience for him to have to await his regiment's mobilisation orders for such a long time, while every day he had to see former comrades of the cadet corps set out on active service with their regiments, to the accompaniment of cheering crowds and the enthusiasm of young and old.

It was therefore somewhat in the nature of a revelation to him when, strolling through the town, we read among the public proclamations a notice from the Inspectorate of the Aviation Corps, which stated that all suitable young men with technical educations could apply to be trained as pilots.

Without wasting many words, we went straight home, where each of us wrote out his own application to the Inspectorate of the Aviation Corps, laying stress on our 'extraordinary technical ability' and our special aptitude for aviation.

It is true that we both had the pleasure of seeing our applications granted, but there was an intolerably long period of waiting for us and our tense, eager expectations. My brother's application did not receive attention until three months later, while mine was held up for seven; meanwhile Max had been called up by his regiment, while I cut a comic figure on the horses of the 48th Dresden Artillery.

31

MOBILISATION AND GARRISON DUTY

On August 18th, 1914, Max received the mobilisation sum-
mons from his old 2nd Railway Regiment in Schöneberg
with a certain satisfaction of knowing his period of inactivi-
ty to be over. He went off to rejoin on the following day.

Not even in his wildest dreams would he have imagined
that the road leading from the last stopping place of the
tramline to the barracks, which he trod on August 19th,
1914, would bear his own name three years later.

After two years of physical and mental work he found his
garrison duties not at all to his taste, for they consisted mainly of supervision and drilling, and the remarks in his letters
concerning his activities are by no means flattering ones. In
any case it is certain that the following three months of garrison service gave him definite confirmation of the fact that
he had done the right thing by terminating his career in the
Railway Regiment two years previously.

I quote from his letters:

"August 21st, 1914.
... Service here is idiotically dull. I am near to my spiritual
death. I have tried everything possible to get away as soon as
I can. But everywhere one finds the same overcrowding and
the same incredible rush to join up. The aviation, railway,
transport and telegraphy corps are all overcrowded. Franz
will have to wait.

I am supposed to live in the town, but I am not doing so.
I am living alone in a fairly big N.C.O.'s room, which was so
dirty that I had to start straight off sweeping and cleaning it
out. I have practically nothing to do in the afternoons, and

then I go out into the town. There is certainly enough work in the mornings, but it is a disgusting idea to be on garrison duty during the war."

"August 26th, 1914.
... All sergeants live in the town. It is not considered the thing to live in barracks. But now, since actually (!) a sword-knot ensign happens to be doing so, a certain sergeant-major belonging to the reserve came to me today and asked if he could share my room. There are two empty beds in it. Well, I don't mind!

I have to show myself in the mess every now and then. When I don't feed there, I send for an ordinary soldier's ration. They usually get helpings in which everything is cooked up together, so that it is easy for me to leave the meat, especially as it is very fat. But naturally I have to put the broth inside me.

Of course there is meat in the mess. I tried living on fruit, but that is too dear, as it comes to at least 2 marks a day, whereas my midday meal in the mess costs only 1.25, and I can eat so much that I don't need any supper.

...Naturally our victories are fine and wonderful things—simply unique—but why should I go to Berlin to exult over them when I have to spend my existence here on garrison duty? I can't help it that our men are so brave."

"Berlin, September 27th, 1914.
I am leading the thoroughly dull life of a hermit, and into the bargain I am in the stupidest thing God ever created—railway service! An inquiry went round as to whether anyone wanted to volunteer for infantry service, and I applied. It is by no means certain that I shall get a transfer to the infantry, but I should certainly like one, for it is really no joke to do

nothing but play the railwaymen's overseer here.

I get quite a lot of riding now. Several officers have noticed that I ride quite decently and entrusted their horses to me. Most of them haven't been ridden at all yet. They have to be taught what to do in response to the various movements of reins and knees. Every morning I ride from two to four different horses from nine to twelve or one, and then I often go to the swimming bath.

Last Thursday they made up another company for active service. I reported to the adjutant and asked why I wasn't included in it. Lieutenant K. said: 'Yes, you're the 1911-12 class; I still have gentlemen of the 1896-97 class here, so your turn is a long way off yet.' Thereupon I explained to him that as a swordknot ensign I was the senior N.C.O. 'Oh Lord, that's right; I never thought of it,' he said. 'Well now, I'll get you a job that will satisfy you until the next active service contingent is made up.' And sure enough it was up in the orders that same evening that I was to be transferred to the 1st Company as acting-officer. The result is that I rank immediately below our lieutenant (because we have no sub-altern) and boss my 'company' about as I like when I drill them in the early morning.

I cannot be promoted to subaltern here, because this is only possible when you are with a regular unit.

As this nomination to acting-officer also carries the advantage that I now draw 110-120 marks a month, it is undoubtedly a reason for acquiring a dog, and I have done so. I have bought Tyras, a German mastiff (of the type that Bismarck used to keep) with a field-grey skin, so big that he can just touch the table with his chin, about a year and a half old and trained as a watchdog—a dear beast. Yesterday I took him out in the Grunewald from 2.30 to 7.30. He is very docile and likes his lessons. He only cost me six marks. I bought him from the Tierasyl, (anmand as I did not know his name, I simply knocked the 'yl' off Tierasyl, so that he is now named Tieras, or, more correctly, Tyras."

"*October 27th, 1914.*
I have somewhat more work with my company; we do socalled 'technical duty' from 8-11 a.m. and from 2-5 p.m. It is terribly futile. My riding is over now, because the horses have gone off on active service already. Tyras has been ill; it was distemper, but I have nursed him through it. Although I am an acting-officer and company-leader, I still live in barracks, but I have the room to myself now. One bed is empty, one is occupied by Tyras, and I sleep in the third. Tyras knows quite well that he mustn't get on the other beds. Of course the brave doggie must go to the war with me, and he's already delighted with the idea!"

This is the last letter written by Max as a 'railwayman'. The Inspectorate of the Aviation Corps dealt with his application of August 8th, and he obtained his transfer at the beginning of November. The joy and enthusiasm with which he commenced work in his new sphere of activity cannot be better depicted than in the words of his next letter.

FIRST FLIGHTS

"*Adlershof, November 16th, 1914.*
You won't realise the great pleasure you gave me with your last parcel. Among the many nice things, for which I send you my heartiest thanks, there was the answer to an application which I made more than three months ago. I shall have

to take you back to the first days of the War to tell the whole story. During those feverish August days it was terrible for me to be still running about at large as a civilian. It was by no means a certainty that my old regiment would call me up in the next few days, because I was definitely not right for an 'operating' company and had not got anything the necessary hang of things to be a success in a 'building' company.

I was in this fix when in the course of a stroll on August 10th I read a proclamation signed by the Inspectorate of the Aviation Corps. This announced that young fellows who wanted to be trained as pilots were to apply at the address given and that those with technical knowledge would have the preference. I put in an application at once, and so did Franz; I sent it off to the Inspectorate, but unfortunately it remained unanswered; from what I heard, there was a terrible crowd wanting to get into the aviation corps. Then on August 12th I was ordered to rejoin my old regiment, and I heard nothing more of my application.

Then you sent me the answer with your last parcel. The Inspectorate wrote: 'Does the applicant still wish to be trained?' I went off at once with my application form to see the adjutant of the Inspectorate and said that I was still as keen on being trained as I was three months ago.

Thus my dearest wish has been fulfilled. On November 12th, 1914, I was posted to the Aviation Replacements Section at Adlershof. I went off on the next day, which was Friday, and now I am installed here as a flying pupil.

So, you see, I got your letter on a Friday, and by the next Thursday I was an airman. I was simply drunk with the joy of having reached my goal.

I reported at the A.R.S. on the Friday and met with an extraordinarily friendly welcome from all concerned.

In the A.R.S. here there is one course of instruction for observers and another for pilots, but only those who have their first and second tests behind them are sent out as pilots.

The military aviation school of Johannistal is right opposite the A.R.S. The pupils here are allotted to the various factories making L.V.G's, Albatroses, Rumplers and Jeanins. The L.V.G's and Albatroses are considered the best.

I have been allotted to the L.V.G. school, and am very pleased. The L.V.G. builds beautiful biplanes which at present give the best results for lift, speed and climbing capacity. For the two days that I have been here I have watched every school flight, but I have not been up yet. My instructor, Herr Kempter, says that we must have better weather for a pupil's first flight.

Today one of the pupils turned right over when he landed, so that the wheels were on top. I was horrified at the sight, but shortly afterwards the pilot crawled out undamaged from under his 'bus'. The older pupils say that sort of thing happens almost every day. So in future I shan't report you such incidents as special events. Apparently that sort of a landing is nothing like so dangerous as it looks.

In order to speed up my training course I am taking part in the instructional classes in Adlershof (engine instruction, aeroplane building, use of the compass, meteorology.) Adlershof is a school for advanced pupils. For the flying itself I have to go with the beginners at Johannistal, of course. I am the only one there who is allowed to go to the classes. I had engine instruction today, but I shan't go to that class again because the man there can teach me nothing new.

Our work begins at 7 a.m., which means getting up at 6.15. There is instruction until 8.30. Flying takes place from 9 a.m.–4 p.m., with a midday interval, of course. Then instruction again from 4.30–6:00 p.m. All the gentlemen here are very nice. The whole tone and the atmosphere around me delights me. All the time you hear the humming and rattling of engines, and wherever you look, you see nothing but engines, cars, motor-bikes, aeroplanes of all types and airships; in short, you are right in the thick of things.

I know very well that you are not in agreement with my step, and that I have not acted according to your views by choosing a life full of dangers instead of one with few risks. But after all I shall survive the war as an airman just as easily as I shall as a railwayman, if Providence has ordained it. Moreover, there has always been this divergence of views between mother and son, as the ancient story of Achilles tells us. But I hope you will find consolation in the fact of knowing I am happy.

Unfortunately, the training will be a fairly long one, according to my instructor—about three months, since by experience the months of November to February have been found unfavourable for school flights. So I shall live in the profoundest peace for another three months. Perhaps the war will be all over by then, and I shall be too late!

I am living in a lovely private house owned by a young married couple. The lady is very nice to Tyras, my big lap-dog.

Is Franz's small car in working order? I could use it here, because I have long tramps every day between Adlershof (classes) and Johannistal (flying)."

"Adlershof, November 20th, 1914.
I made several ascents today with my instructor. Four of them, altogether. Flying is a remarkable business. I think the finest moment is the one when you leave the ground. All the

jolting stops then. Going into a glide is less pleasant; it is like being in a lift. The instructor never flies high when he has pupils—about 50-80 metres up.

Today was a glorious autumn day, and so activities were lively. Suddenly all aeroplanes were forbidden to take off. The Zeppelin was brought out of its shed and went up twenty minutes later. I have never seen a Z. Ship in such close proximity.

Life is always busy on the aerodrome; sometimes there are ten or more machines in the air, and the Schütte-Lanz and a Zeppelin as well. One hardly bothers to look at them."

THE FLYING SCHOOL

"Adlershof, December 2nd, 1914.
It is surprising that time positively flies for us airmen? Or is it really not so long ago since you wrote to me last? To me it seems an eternity. And as a matter of fact it is nine days, and when staid Age does not write for nine days, it is the same as if frivolous Youth did not take up a pen for nine weeks. By the way, you really need not worry if you remain for a long time without news of me, for firstly: on principle, no news is good news, and secondly: in the case of an accident, the authorities here would inform you at once. But you need not worry, for in an aeroplane one feels at least as safe as in an armchair on the ground, and ten times as happy into the bargain!

Thanks to the good weather of the last few days, our instruction has progressed gaily. I have now been in the air twenty times. Unfortunately, I do not notice any increase in my ability. I have been piloting ever since the sixth ascent.

The business is not at all dangerous and not so hard as I imagined, but you have to look out when you land. Naturally, I cannot say yet whether I shall remain in aviation. Flying is splendid. You never feel it's not safe. It is far more exciting than in a car. The glorious peace in the air—and—no policeman! I have been given the controls fairly early; many pupils do not get them until after the twelfth to fifteenth flight.

You ask why we fly so low when we are learning—only about 50 metres up. I believe the main reason is that they do not want to waste time in long climbs involving several spirals, but prefer to give as many opportunities as possible for landings, because these are the most difficult of all. When learning, we never go up any higher than we do on the first flights. There is reason for it, because it is all the same whether you sail about at 50 or 500 metres up. On the other hand, you are often better off higher up, because if the machine drops down from 500 metres you have sufficient time to right it again, while at 50 metres the time is too short for you to do anything. But a fall from 500 metres lasts ten seconds, so that you have time enough to sing 'Heil Dir im Siegerkranz' and give three cheers for the Emperor.

Generally the men stick in their machines when they crash and climb out when the crash is over. Then they go off to the factory and report: 'Done is done and gone is gone and crashed is crashed'—then they sing the lovely song, 'Off we go, off we go' (along the ground) 'that is not so hard, you know' (above the aerodrome), and when they crash down, they continue the song: 'We want to have another game, because we didn't find it time.'

Still the instruction doesn't always go on so smoothly. Two crashed to their deaths yesterday; you will have read

about it in the paper. Eyewitnesses say that the pilot made
the mistake of trying to climb on a turn, and so the machine
sideslipped. Comparatively few machines are smashed up
altogether when bad landings occur; all the same you learn
rather more than you want to when you damage the
machine slightly. Of course, no machines are flown unless
they are in perfect working order.

I don't pay a single pfennig's tax on Tyras. He has got a
label on his collar, inscribed: 'War dog.' And that's that.

Ask all the questions you like, or—better still—come and
see me here, because lengthy letters take such a lot of time."

"Adlershof, December 29th, 1914.

My journey to Berlin was not pleasant. The carriages
were swinishly cold. I had to wait nearly two hours in Riesa
and change at Röderau. I was back in Berlin at 9. There was
no instruction, because it was very gusty. One fellow crashed
today; the machine was smashed up. The man was hardly
hurt. (A Jeanin Monoplane.) Yesterday a Rumpler biplane
crashed; observer dead, pilot injured. Very bad weather
today. The snow has gone again.

Ilse Boetzel wrote to me to fly over her place and drop a
bomb. Thereupon I sent her a chocolate air-bomb.

That was a lovely Christmas! Once again, heartiest
thanks for everything. Naturally, I haven't much to tell you
today, because nothing has happened."

FIRST AND SECOND TESTS

"Adlershof, February 14th, 1915.

Having told you so much when I spent Christmas in
Dresden, it is not until today that I have anything further to

recount. After a period of terrible weather from the middle of December to the middle of January we started a round of fine days again, so that I was once more able to make some small progress. After a fairly large number of instructional flights (54 in all) my instructor let me go up alone for the first time on January 31st. My first solo flight went off well, and with it my confidence in the success of further flights was considerably strengthened.

I fulfilled all the necessary conditions in quick succession, and on February 9th I passed my pilot's tests. All I had to do was to go up, fly five figures of eight, and then land on the spot where the instructor stood with his red flag, go up again, fly another five figures of eight and land as before. Finally I had to climb to at least 100 metres and land in a glide. These conditions were soon fulfilled, and then I was able to tackle the preliminary tests required of a war pilot.

They were: 20 smooth landings, two flights of half an hour each at 500 meters, and then the actual war pilot's tests of a flight of an hour at 2,000 metres and a glide down from 800 metres. I did the twenty landings all on one day and on the next the half hour flight (at 650 metres); on February 11th, the third day, I did the other half hour flight and followed it up with the field pilot's tests. I kept on climbing and reached 2,600 metres, which is the record (for a pupil) since the existence of the school. Instead of an hour I stayed up for an hour and twenty minutes, and instead of a glide from 800 metres I did one from 2,200. During such flights you carry a 'barograph', which records exactly your climbs and drops, the heights at which you fly and start to glide.

The times for my climb and descent were:

1,000 metres in 12 minutes.

2,000 in 40 minutes.

2,600 in 1 hour and 5 minutes.

Then a short drop to 2,400.

Then a straight flight of 20 minutes.

Then a glide of 3 minutes from 2,200 metres.

My instructor was very satisfied with the business. Having passed my war pilot's tests, I have finished my time at the Johannistal Flying School and have been passed on to the A.R.S. 2, Adlershof, for further instruction."

THE FIRST CRASH

"Adlershof, March 1st, 1915.

Another fortnight has passed since my last letter.

When I was transferred to Adlershof on February 12th, there were already a lot of pupils there, who all had the same goal before their eyes—the third tests. But unfortunately there were only very few machines at our disposal, so that the training was likely to be a lengthy matter. One had to reckon with anything from four to six weeks. After waiting a fortnight, i.e. at the end of February, I had fulfilled all the preliminary requirements for the third tests with the exception of the two short cross-country flights. I made about 45 flights under varying conditions.

One day a certain Lieutenant von Pannewitz came here from the front to pick two new pilots for his section. He asked who were the best, and my name was promptly given to him first. When he heard I had not yet done any cross-country flights, he was very sorry. Then he asked me if I was ready to go to Verdun with him on Monday. I naturally said yes. But he finally acquired misgivings about taking me straight off and made my transfer dependant on two conditions: (1) I was to give him a demonstration of a landing from 800 metres. (2) I was to make a landing on rough ground.

I fulfilled the first condition to his complete satisfaction by making a couple of neat spirals in the course of my glide. When I tried the second landing, the machine got a nasty jolt from a heap of manure, which bounced it up again, and then it turned over with me inside. Luckily I was strapped in; otherwise I should have gone down underneath the machine and been crushed. But as it was I got off fairly lightly.

I had a strange feeling at the moment when I turned over, although an upside down position (without a machine) is nothing new to me. If I had switched the engine on again, I should have avoided the crash.

While I worked my way forward under the wreckage, I thought to myself: 'Well, the lieutenant will think twice about taking you,' and so it came to pass. When I was clear of the machine, I had to look at the damage, and then I saw the consequences of my landing—propeller, undercarriage and left wing smashed, fuselage crumpled up, in short, 'bus total write off'.

Naturally my job at the front was off. I was received on the tarmac with well meant advice to practise landings diligently etc.

Now I can sit at home several weeks more, for certain! But that's the way of it: I have 130 smooth landings to my credit, and for the 131st, on which everything depends, I make a crash. All the same I have the reputation of being a good pilot. That reputation has not suffered by the crash. Everyone consoled me by saying that that sort of thing could happen to the biggest guns.

Now I have made the best of it and got used to the idea

of stopping here some time longer. For my third tests I have to do fifteen landings outside the aerodrome, two flights to Döberitz and a long cross-country flight. The latter's destination must naturally be an aerodrome, so that Brunswick won't do. Dresden, Grossenhain, Leipzig and Hannover are possibilities. Leipzig is generally chosen. Bad weather has set in now, and will last for several days. All the same I hope to be through by the middle of March."

THE AIRCRAFT PARK

"Rethel, March 14th, 1915.
Having reached my destination and got more or less straight there, I shall now tell you something about the events of last week. A telegram arrived on March 4th: 'Send two pilots at once to Army Aircraft Park 3'. Contrary to my expectation, I was chosen once more. I was told the same day, but I was by no means ready to travel. I found the most varied opinions about the words 'at once' in the telegram. Some thought I would have to go off the next day, while others said I had at least three days grace.

All the same I had to make haste. I ran off to the paymaster to get the money to which I was entitled for my active service outfit. He maintained that I should draw that at the front. That did not seem right, and later it was shown to be wrong, for what use would the outfit money be to me at the front? However, I did not get any cash from him, and finally I borrowed it from Herr Karow.

As soon as I had the money, I did some feverish shopping; there were also all sorts of things to do, such as farewell visits, packing up, drawing clothing from the store, getting papers and tickets made out, etc. Gradually I began to notice that the business was really not so urgent, and so I finally allowed myself a bit more time.

At last, on Tuesday, I was far enough advanced to report myself ready to start. During the last months I have had a glorious life in Adlershof. In fact, I was very popular, and with my superiors as well as with comrades and subordinates. When I made my crash, there was not the slightest sign of any malicious glee, as was so often the case with the others. When it was given out (on March 3rd) that I was in charge of all the other pilots (as regards service, uniform, quarters, leave and extra-service occupations) a general 'Bravo!' echoed through the ranks. Unfortunately the order which summoned me away came the next day. My instructor and the captain in charge of service on the aerodrome were full of my praise. After I left, he praised me again in front of all the other airmen, as Franz and I heard later on. Briefly, I was sorry in some respects to leave the place where I had made a pleasant position for myself, with really great interest and much love for the service there. One consoling thought was that I was likely to succeed in giving satisfaction to my superiors in my new sphere of work.

It was left to me to start off when I pleased. I left Adlershof on the Tuesday in time to catch the 8 p.m. express to Cologne. My hostess was very loath to let my good Tyras depart. In the evening I left the Friedrichstrasse Station, Berlin, for Cologne, after first meeting Franz. The poor fellow did not enjoy his leave particularly; my shopping must have bored him considerably. The following morning I was in Cologne at 8.30 a.m., and my next train did not leave till noon. I strolled through the town; later I travelled on in the direction of Herbesthal, reaching Liège in the afternoon

(Wednesday), and left again (on Thursday) for Namur, Maubeuge and St. Quentin, reaching Tergnier finally at about 11 a.m. I then went on to Charleville, via Laon, where I had a wait from 1 a.m. to 6 a.m., after which came the final stage to Rethel, which I reached about 10 a.m. So I arrived on Friday, the 12th. My good Tyras made the whole journey with me. During the trip I saw fewer signs of war than I expected; a few bridges which had been blown up were the only things to remind one of past fighting. The railway construction company has rebuilt some of the bridges perfectly, while others have been replaced by new ones. From the station I telephoned for a car to take me to the aircraft park three kilometres away. We drove through Rethel, which was badly shot about. The centre of the town is a huge heap of ruins.

The road begins to rise somewhat outside the town. The aerodrome is on the slope to the left, while the one on the right is surmounted by a little white château, with a park. This is used for the officers' quarters and mess. If you continue along the road from Rethel, you find it dipping somewhat and then climbing again. In the declivity there is a small ruined village, which is almost completely deserted; only ten old inhabitants have remained. On the next rise there is a farm, which is mainly used as quarters for the men. I have been accommodated in the 'gentlemen's house'. The farm looks very picturesque and beautiful when viewed from the château. The whole district, forming part of the Aisne valley, is a series of gentle hills. As far as the eye reaches, there are only fields and meadows to be seen—no woods.

From a close view the farm does not make a very favourable impression. I am the farmer. On the farm I have from 30-40 men under me, mainly lorry-drivers and mechanics. There are a number of lorries belonging to our section, for the use and supervision of which I am responsible. So there is a job I can do. 'My' farm includes a dwelling-house, in which are the men's rooms, my room and the kitchen. Then there are four huge sheds, which house cars, aeroplanes and spare parts. In addition to these there is a brandy still (not operating), stables for twelve horses, byres for cows and sheep, pigsties and chicken-houses. I cannot imagine anything better than I have here. The weather is mild, but unfortunately very misty. My activities consist of flying and driving a car. The first is a very frequent one, because I am going to catch up with my third tests here.

Our whole life here is very peaceable. It is only a pity that the houses have been so much knocked to pieces. This fact and the large numbers of soldiers one sees here are the only things which remind one of the war. Yesterday and today there were heavy bombardments in the direction of Rheims. They sounded like distant thunder.

The mechanical side of me has come into its own here. I am planted right in the middle of engines, so to speak. Either I ride a motor-cycle, of which we have three, or drive a car or fly. We have here L.V.G.s, Albatroses and Gotha-Taubes. I fly an L.V.G. Unfortunately, although the weather is calm, the visibility is not good enough to go high. Today I was so much in the clouds at 300 metres that I could not see the ground. Naturally I went down again hastily, because it is an extremely unpleasant feeling.

As I am the leader of the lorry column, I have to make a trip of at least 40 kilometres once a month. Where I take the column is my affair. I shall return to this subject later. When on duty, I use either a car or a motor cycle, and if I go anywhere on pleasure bent, I can always tack a duty on to the trip. My only private jaunts are when I ride or drive from the château to the farm (a whole kilometre). I shall try to give you some sort of a picture of my farm. I think you will have a fair idea of my activities from what I have already written. I need hardly say how much I like them.

As regards food, we are completely dependent on the mess, because we can buy nothing in the town. Unfortunately very few fresh vegetables are seen on our table. An enrichment of the menu by means of kind gifts (for example, tinned vegetables, such as asparagus, beans, mushrooms and spinach) would therefore be always heartily welcome. As extras I should recommend plain chocolate, biscuits, Freiburg bretzels and finally a few cigarettes. I do not smoke myself, but my batman does, and he feeds Tyras so well. Now he has got bad paws (the dog—not the batman), but he doesn't touch the chickens (I mean the dog again). He feels very happy as a farm-dog. The batman is a splendid fellow. I am afraid he spoils me. Yesterday he decorated my room with the first violets he plucked.

It is certainly not necessary to send the men here any woollen things, for in the first place winter is over and in the second they are all well provided with blankets and everything they need; in fact they are well equipped in every respect because the section has been stationed here half a year. But everyone is glad to receive something to eat and smoke.

While writing this letter, I have just received your last card. So there's a nine milliard war loan! That is splendid! It seems to have gone down all right this time without my money. But the next time I'll subscribe too!

Prince Oscar of Prussia is supposed to be visiting us tomorrow.

No flying weather today. The day passed very wearily. Nothing happened except that Tyras fell off the sofa backwards. He was very surprised and displeased at his fall.

One of our pigs was slaughtered this evening.

Poor piggy!

Now there are only three of them!"

"Rethel, March 25th, 1915.

After a run of bad days there was glorious flying weather on March 21st, so that I went up gaily again; I visited Sections 22 and 53 and brought them their mail and spare parts. The weather was splendid. I flew about 100 kilometres.

The weather was just as fine on Monday, March 22nd. I had to utilise it. I went up about 10 a.m., to fly my observer to Section 13, to which he has been transferred. We made an intentional detour in order to fly longer. We greeted Section 22 from aloft and then made for Section 13. When we were about to land at this Section's aerodrome, we got into the German anti-balloon artillery's* fire, which was meant for a French machine. Not until after a long, long search did I discover a French biplane about 600 metres above us. We were 1,400 metres up, but he was 2,000. It is the first time I have seen an aeroplane under fire. The little shrapnel clouds looked charming. The Frenchman then flew on to Rethel. We landed in Pont Faverger and learnt that the Frenchman had dropped two bombs on the railway station there, with the usual lack of success. I put my observer down and reached my home aerodrome alone about 12.30 a.m.

In the afternoon I got into my car—a little French 6/16 h.p. one—and started my column off on one of the practice tours I have already mentioned to you. I could take them where I liked, and chose a 60 kilometre round. Naturally we made a slow pace with the lorries. I kept on whirling round

* For the first year of the war the German anti-aircraft batteries were still known as anti-balloon artillery. Translator's Note

and round the column like a sheep-dog. We landed back again in Resson about 6.30 p.m., without any hitches or hold-ups. A sergeant (my right-hand man) said no trip had ever gone off so smoothly; usually there were a number of hold-ups. And I can say that it was a great pleasure to see how well they all drove, and they did so because they saw the trouble I took to make the trip a success. I was all dusty and thoroughly tired when I got back.

On March 23rd it rained until about 10 a.m. About 10.30 a captain—whose name I cannot remember—came to see his nephew, who is doing duty with us as a lorry-driver. I took our guest round and showed him the farm, the château and the aerodrome. Then I drove him and his nephew, who had obtained leave, in a 50 h.p. Itala car (a huge covered Italian car) first to the château and then into Rethel. He refused my offer to take him up for a short flight, saying that he was the father of four children. After lunch I went to fetch them both—in a small, open Bergmann car this time. When we reached the aerodrome, he said: 'I shall certainly never again in my life get another offer of a flight,' and asked whether I would permit him to fly in spite of his wife and children. After declining all responsibility, I declared myself ready to take him up.

Then I rocked about in the air for an hour with this gentleman! It was the loveliest flight I have ever made. We climbed above the clouds at 2,000 metres. A radiantly bright sun shone down on the thick white masses of cloud. We only saw the ground every now and then through holes in the clouds. It was a glorious sensation to be sailing the ocean of air without seeing the earth or being seen from the earth. Then suddenly another machine broke through the clouds on our right. It was also an L.V.G., probably belonging to

Section 22, for I estimated that we must be somewhere over Vouziers aerodrome. Shortly afterwards, as a matter of fact, I saw the Aisne gleaming through a gap in the clouds, and Vouziers lies on that river. I therefore turned back, because the French positions are not far away from Vouziers. On the way home the captain tried to make me understand by his gestures what a wonderful experience the flight was for him. Twenty minutes later I pushed down through the clouds and saw our hangars about 1,000 metres below us. The gentleman clapped his hands over his ears during our glide down, because the buzzing was too much for him.

When we were on the ground again, he was still quite overwhelmed with the impressions of his flight. He declared it was the next best day of his life to the one on which he got engaged and said: 'To think that I nearly missed this glorious spectacle!' Then he added: 'Well, you know, when we were in the car, I was so amazed at the quiet and safe way you handled it, and then I thought to myself: "You can trust yourself in the air with that man!" '

He was full of gratitude when he departed. Then I went up again—this time with our newly arrived observer. We wanted to climb to 1,000 metres, but ran into rain at 800 and so went down again.

Yesterday we combined business and pleasure most neatly. An officer had to go to Charleville on service affairs. The vacant seats in the Itala were occupied by several men who wanted a jaunt, and among them was myself. We left at noon and reached Charleville at 2.30. While the officer was doing his business, we had a look at the place. Afterwards we drove to Bazeilles, via Sedan, to see the catacombs. These are the huge vaults in which many who fell in 1870 found their last resting-places. They are not buried, but the bones are piled up in layers and the skulls set out in rows. It was very praiseworthy of the people to give the dead such a worthy grave, but I cannot understand why anyone is allowed to visit these catacombs for a 'pourboire'.

On our way back to Rethel we passed the house in Donchery where Bismarck negotiated with the French emperor. It is a modest little house, which also bears signs of this war. One of its walls was shot through several times, and a bullet hit a vase standing on the mantelpiece. The historic room brings the owner's wife quite a handsome little sum of money. We got home at last at about 7 p.m.

In reply to your question: 'What is Prince Oscar doing with us?' Well, we are certainly airmen, but we have preserved our humility and are therefore pleased to invite folk who are not airmen. We are indeed very affable with our comrades. We have someone to visit us almost every day.

What is a brigade, you ask. A brigade belongs to a division, for two brigades form a division. The military structures are built downwards:

The national army consists of various armies.

Each army consists of two army corps.

Each army corps consists of two infantry divisions (with cavalry, artillery, pioneers, railwaymen, transport, airmen and wireless).

Each division consists of two brigades.

Each brigade of three regiments.

Each regiment of three battalions.

Each battalion of four companies.

Each company of three platoons.

There was no flying weather all yesterday; today, too, it has been raining and blowing all the time. An excellent day for letter-writing.

I do not agree with the final sentence of your letter. And I am not alone, because all the German armed forces are with me. I mean your sentence: 'We are not fighting for victory, but for peace.' No! We are fighting for victory, because there can be no peace without victory. For what should we Germans do with a peace without victory? History shows plainly how long such a peace would last. A peace without victory will last seven years at the most, while a victorious peace will last over forty years. We are therefore fighting for a victorious peace.

Now I am afraid that with this long letter I shall have given you hopes that all my letters will be as long. So no false hopes, please."

THE THIRD TESTS

"*Rethel, March 31st, 1915.*
I am sorry I have not been able to write for several days. On the whole, nothing has happened, except that I have my third tests behind me. I will tell you all about this flight.

I took off on Saturday, March 27th, to fly to Brussels. Equipped with maps, my observer put us on a due north course. About 10 a.m. I had climbed up to 2,560 metres; I flew on at this height. After I had flown for an hour, the clouds which lay between 1,000 and 1,200 metres grew so thick that we could only see the ground occasionally. To make matters worse, the engine began to give out. Judging by the clock, I thought we ought to be in Brussels, and therefore dropped down through the clouds to 1,200. There was a big town below us, which seemed as if it might be Hal—a place to the south of Brussels. Some while later, when we ought to have sighted Brussels, my petrol ran out, and the engine got worse and worse. I therefore decided to make a forced landing.

From 1,000 metres up I spied a field, which seemed suitable; I throttled the engine down, went into a glide and circled round the field at 100 metres, in order to have a look at it. Then I put the machine down cunningly on the spot I had chosen. The landing came off quite smoothly. Everything was all right.

The first question was: where were we? Behind us, on our right, there was a village, with the railway running by it. I had seen it from above. Several peasants came along, and soon afterwards some children, boys and girls. From afar we heard their shouts of joy: 'Il est tombé!'

But he had not tombé. In my best French I asked one of the peasants:

'Le nom de ce village?'

'Lihrsnohr.' (At least, that was what it sounded like.)

'Combien de kilomètres jusqu'à Bruxelles?'

'C'est très loin encore.'

'Quelle grande ville est située dans cette direction?' (The town over which I had flown.)

'C'est Courtrai.' We looked up Courtrai on our map I: ' Y a-t-il de l'essence ici?'

'Il n'y a pas, mais à Courtrai.'

'Combien de kilomètres à Courtrai?'

'Quatorze.'

'Y a-t-il une automobile, bicyclette, une voiture?'

'Rien de tout!'

'Quelle ville est la plus prochaine d'ici?'

'Roubaix, dix kilomètres.'

Well, at last we got enough out of them to gather we had

lost our way completely. My observer got his direction wrong when we were over the clouds. We had flown too far west and were only 20 kilometres away from Lille. Our astonishment was not little. Soon, however, some German Landsturmers and railwaymen came along, having seen us land from afar. We had come down at Estampuis, and the next station was Leers-Nord. In their mixed French and Flemish dialect the villagers called it 'Lihrsnohr'.

I went to the railway station, where I telephoned to Rethel to inform my section-commander and to Courtrai for petrol. Meanwhile about two or three hundred people had congregated round the machine. We put several Landsturmers on guard over it and then gratefully accepted the invitation of the lieutenant who was commandant of Estampuis to lunch with him.

At 4 p.m. 100 litres of petrol arrived.

At last, at 5 p.m., we were ready to take off. We flew to Lille aerodrome, which we found after a bit of a search. Just as the machine was taxi-ing along the ground, she I was lifted up again by a ground-gust. A knock from the wind caught her broadside on, and crack! when we came down again, we broke both wheels and a strut of the undercarriage. Our great bird lay lame in the field. We had landed on Section 24's aerodrome. Unfortunately, they had no L.V.G. parts; we had to go round to Section 5 b to get the necessary spares. Our bird was ready again the next day, but we gave up the idea of taking off because of the strong headwind, and did not start back again till Monday.

Lille is quite a pretty town, but parts of it have been badly shot about. Unfortunately, I did not see much of it, because I was looking after the machine. We went off home at 8.30 a.m. on Monday, but I have never been so tossed about as I was that day. With the greatest difficulty I climbed up above the clouds to 2,000 metres, where it was calm. We reached Rethel after a two and a half hours' flight. It was damnably cold. My right hand was quite numb. Then I ended by making a bad landing in Rethel, but without any damage. The distance as the crow flies was 350 kilometres, but we certainly flew 400. Feeling thankful that the flight had ended so well, I saw myself in my mind's eye already decorated with the pilot's badge which according to the regulations is conferred after these so-called tests.

Today (March 31st), at 5 a.m., they are going to unveil a statue in Rethel in honour of Bismarck's 100 birthday, and I mean to have a look at the ceremony from above.

I flew over the place and my observer photographed the ceremony from 400 metres up."

AN EXPERIENCE

"Rethel, April 6th, 1915.
I have not flown since my last letter. That really seems incredible. But the April weather is horrible; there is snow, rain, hail, wind and sunshine alternately.

We had a fine experience on the third Easter holiday. I had just arrived with our Itala car, which was crammed full of gentlemen from Section 13 in 'Bongt Fawarcher', as our Saxons call Pont Faverger, and we were sitting in the mess with strong coffee when suddenly the alarm went: 'Enemy aircraft!' We heard the drone of a machine but in view of the bad weather could not believe it to be an enemy one. The sergeant-major got hold of a few men and commanded them to get their rifles.

When we went out into the road, we actually saw a French biplane at a low height, about 250 metres up, flying over the château in the direction of the farm. It was already too far away for a shot. When it got to the farm, it turned round, headed for the aerodrome and went into a glide. We naturally did not fire when we saw that, but everyone lay down flat on his stomach in case the enemy was going to shoot. Suddenly I found I was the only one still standing upright, for firstly I did not think he would shoot, and secondly the ground was too dirty for me.

The Frenchman made a perfect landing on our aerodrome, and we went up to him as soon as his machine stopped. In it sat two men, both of whom raised their hands to heaven as a sign that they meant to offer no resistance. They were taken prisoners and escorted in triumph to the mess, where we invited them to coffee.

Their story was as follows:

There is a factory at Le Bourget, near Paris, and our prisoners were detailed to fly a new machine from it to Châlons-sur-Marne, but were driven out of their course by a strong wind, and as their map only showed the country as far as Rheims, they lost their way.

When the pilot saw our aerodrome, he thought he was over Châlons; he mistook the Aisne for the Marne and so he landed, thinking he was still on the French side of the line. He was not a little horrified when he suddenly saw German soldiers around him. Luckily he knew it was useless to offer resistance, and so resigned himself to his fate at once. But we can easily imagine his shock.

After he had told us many interesting things, we sent him on to G.H.Q. Thus we became the owners of a brand new machine, a small Caudron biplane. C'est la guerre!"

THE FRONT, AT LAST!

(Artillery observation flier from April 13th–25th, 1915.)

"Vrizy, near Vouziers, April 21st, 1915.
Before I deal with the questions in your letter, I want to describe my experiences of last week, which will give you the answers to several of them automatically.

There is a gap of several days in my report on events in Rethel. I did not fly at all up to April 11th. April 12th was the first fine day for a long time.

For several days it had been a question whether I should be transferred to Section 10 or 13. On the 12th it was decided that I was to go to No. 10, in Vrizy. My transfer came very suddenly, because one of Section 10's pilots fell ill.

I took off at 2 p.m., in order to reach my new destination by air. My batman took dog and luggage on a lorry. As a beginner, I did not find it at all easy to spot an aerodrome I had not yet seen from a height of 2,000 metres, and it was only after a long search that I spied the section's sheds. My arrival was expected, and they fired some signal lights to help me find the place. I had only just landed when the lorry arrived with my 'belongings'.

As the gentleman whose place I was taking had not left yet, I had to find provisional accommodation. I made the acquaintance of the section's officers in the mess; my observer was Lieutenant Bissmeyer, a former artilleryman, who has been with the section since last October.

We went off to the aerodrome in the afternoon. It lies on a rise, about a kilometre away from the village, and was an aerodrome before the war. The hangars which were built in peacetime now house our birds.

When we reached the aerodrome, the men were busy putting my machine right for active service. They laid metal sheets under the tank and under the two seats, and fixed racks to store the bombs, a map-board, an altimeter and a few other gadgets.

We had planned to go up that same afternoon, but had to drop the idea on account of the work in progress.

It was not finished until the next day, and we took off about 11 a.m. My observer wanted to show me round, so we flew up to our trenches and then along them at a height of 2,000 metres. It is amazing how accurately you see each trench, and even each shell-hole. The whole countryside has been terribly torn up, and all buildings shot to pieces. One learns what it really means to have the war in one's country. You don't see a single town or village. All have been burnt and shot to pieces. The country round Perthes looks the worst.

We returned after a flight of an hour and a half. When I landed, the same thing happened to me as in Lille, i.e., the forward right strut of the undercarriage and a wheel broke off. I was inconsolable about my bad luck and clumsiness, but all the officers comforted me; that sort of thing was part of flying, they said, and not at all surprising, considering the bad state of the aerodrome.

It took a day and a half to put the damage right. To ensure greater solidity, they filled the struts (which were originally hollow) up with wood. They took the wings off during the repairs, so as to work more comfortably. Whether they did not brace them right when they put them on again or whether the new struts were too heavy, I cannot say, but the fact remains that it was impossible to get any higher than 1,500 metres, which is not high enough for active service.

I therefore received orders to get a new machine from Rethel; my observer and I obeyed them the next day and came back at 6 p.m. with the new machine, which can at least climb to 2,400 or 2,600, even if it is a bit slow.

When I landed the new machine, I touched the ground with my left wing. A strut between the upper and lower wings gave way, but the damage was mended in ten minutes. Since that time I have at last managed to make decent landings again, as I used to do before. My list of breakages has therewith risen to three, with a small fracture as well.

ARTILLERY OBSERVATION FLIER IN THE CHAMPAGNE

One day my observer received orders that we were to spot for the artillery, i.e. to observe the shooting of the artillery from the air and correct the range from our observations by an agreed code of signals and by our reports and sketches. We therefore had to get into touch with the commander of the artillery section in question.

So we chose a nice, fine morning and flew off to a flying section with an aerodrome somewhat nearer the front than our own. We lunched there, and then went on to Maure by car. There they saddled two horses for us, and gave us a mounted guide, because it was impossible to make any further progress by car along a road which had been so heavily shelled. Our guide was very helpful, for without him I do not think we could have found the artillery positions, because they were so well concealed. Moreover he knew exactly the parts of the road which were under enemy fire.

We passed numerous shell-holes at a gallop. At last, after

a couple of hours on horseback, we reached our destination. After half an hour's conference, we rode back, and escaped being hit on the return trip. Then we continued our journey by car to the aerodrome, entered our machine and flew home. After making a good landing we went into the mess— very hungry. I had not been on a horse's back for six months, and then, all of a sudden, this four hours' ride! I felt very done up, and decided that flying is the only fit and proper occupation.

The next day we started spotting for Section 2 of the 99th Artillery Regiment. We give our directions by means of signal lights which burn so brightly that they are visible by daylight. We have to do this job every day now, and once or twice a day. Generally our flights pass off very smoothly; it doesn't worry us much when we are shot at, but yesterday we had an unpleasant experience. We took off at 5.50 a.m., and at 6.30 we were about 2,200 metres up—a height which suffices to give a perfect view of the artillery's fire. We flew southwards to Le Mesnil, and were shelled very heavily, more heavily than ever before. I turned and flew towards Tahure. We saw the dainty little clouds appear on our right and left, above and below us. In order to dodge them I went into a sharp left-hand turn, which was a bit too sharp. I made the mistake of oversteering my machine, which promptly started to sideslip, and then plunged into the depths with the engine full on. It kept on revolving from right to left like a top, and the rev-counter showed 1,600 revolutions a minute (1,400 is the normal). It did not occur to me at once that it was my fault, but I thought my elevator had been carried away by a shrapnel, the bursting of which I had heard faintly.

After a comparatively long delay I moved the controls

instinctively (right rudder and full right aileron); then the spinning movement came to an end and the machine assumed a normal position again. So everything seemed to be still in order. I pulled the stick slightly, and the machine began to climb.

It was some time before my observer found our whereabouts. We were flying at 1,700 metres, having thus fallen 500 in a few seconds. I was in a fright at the moment when we began to fall, but I said to myself at once that I had a lot of time before we reached the ground, because we were 2,200 metres up, and even a falling stone would take 21 seconds to get down from such a height. Well, the fall of an aeroplane was bound to take longer than that of a stone, because of the resistance offered by the wings. It would last a minute or longer.

When we got home, we were happy about the incident. The artillery commander, who had noticed our spin, telephoned to ask if anyone was hurt, which we were luckily able to deny.

The day before that experience we located a new French battery, whereupon we went off to G.H.Q. by car to report it. We ran straight into the arms of the general in command, so that we could tell him our tale at once. Apart from that nothing has happened. We have plenty to do, but today is a day of rest, because it is raining."

"Vrizy, end of April, 1915.
I told you in my last letter that I was accommodated with provisional quarters. I was able to leave them two days later. Now I am living in a pretty little villa, which is five minutes walk from the mess and ten from the aerodrome. There is a lieutenant living there as well, and our batmen.

Vrizy is in a pretty locality, but the village itself is very dirty like all French villages are (also in peacetime).

We are ten officers altogether—one section-commander, four pilots and five observers. The gentlemen are all very nice, but that is a matter of course with airmen.

One day's work was as follows: 8 a.m. breakfast, 9 a.m. on the aerodrome, 10-12 flying, 1 p.m. lunch, on the aerodrome again, at 2 and tinkering with the machine till 4. 4.30—6.30 p.m. flying.

We often have conferences with the artillery people in the afternoon instead of flying, in which case we have to go to Maure by car.

If Franz comes out as an artilleryman, it may happen by chance that we direct the battery he belongs to.

And now to answer your letter of April 15th:

I am not at all sorry to be away from Rethel; it was quite nice there, but terribly peaceful. From the very beginning it was clearly only a transitional station for me until there was a chance to get into a Flying Section.

You ask why there are so many men in Rethel and whether they are used. Well, they are there because they can be used there, and the 130 men are employed as follows: 60 drivers of lorries and cars, 10 brakesmen on attached vehicles, 15 mechanics, 5 locksmiths, 2 carpenters, 3 cabinet-makers, 5 cooks, 10 men in the harness-room, 5 batmen and 15 N.C.O.s.

My observer in Rethel was quite a beginner, which is the reason why we lost our way on the trip about which I wrote you on March 31st. Naturally the pilot steers the machine, but as such he has all sorts of things to attend to, as for instance, right rudder, left rudder, right aileron, left aileron, and elevator, in addition to watching the revcounter, the compass and the petrol and oil gauges, listening to the engine and keeping an eye on the machine. Consequently it is quite pleasant to have a man with you who can compare the ground below with a map and then tell you by a gesture whether to steer right or left in order to reach your goal. We call such a man the observer.

Tyras's complaint was not foot and mouth disease. You don't seem to be quite up in your 'geography', for otherwise you would know that only animals which walk on their hoofs and not on the pad of the foot, as Tyras does, can get foot and mouth disease. Tyras stepped into some acid that had run out from an accumulator, and it ate away his skin.

I have received the press-cutting entitled 'The Air Mail on Active Service'; heartiest thanks for the same. The person in question has written a lot of silly rot, but it amuses us all to read that sort of nonsense. However, the high-flown words which turn quite an ordinary action into a heroic achievement are in no way fitting for the honourable trade of flying. An airman flies—he does not drive. Consequently he does not make reconnaissance rides, but reconnaissance flights.

In case of anything happening to me, my batman has precise instructions what to do.

I have not grown fatter, even in the cheeks, but I am clean shaven, and my hair has been cut 'en brousse'. With no parting the hairs are 3 millimetres long, and naturally look like a lavatory brush."

FLYING SECTION 62—THE NEW HOME

After a 'guest-performance' of only thirteen days with Flying Section 10, which was his first introduction to war flying,

my brother was transferred to Döberitz, to join the new
Flying Section 62, which was in process of formation.

This transfer to a new section could not be anything but
agreeable to him as a young pilot, because, as we perceive
from his letters, it is easier to grow into the life of a completely new section, in which all the members have got to
make each other's acquaintance, than for a novice to enter
the solid structure of a section which has already gained its
own experience of war. Naturally this new section was not
recruited entirely from young airmen, such as pilots who had
only just passed their third tests or observers who were only
just through the observers' course and therefore had as little
experience of the front as my brother or none at all. To it
were also allotted several experienced observers and pilots,
as, for example, Lieutenant Boelcke, who had been already
seven months at the front.

My brother's affable disposition soon won him a general
popularity, but he formed a particularly close friendship
with Lieutenant Boelcke during his first days in the section.
Not only had he a common bond with Boelcke in their
mutual love of flying, but they were also drawn together by
similar traits and outlooks. The fact that my brother
acknowledged without jealousy (and as something self-evi-
dent) the privileged position which Boelcke enjoyed in the
section as a pre-war pilot, as well as an experienced war one,
may well have contributed to the establishment of a friendship between these two, which soon exceeded the type of
intimacy formed by the common bond of the war experiences that was to be theirs so soon.

The quick rise of my brother and the fact that Section 62
soon excelled all other sections were both largely due to the
circumstance that it was led by an experienced airman,

Captain Kastner. The latter soon gave much attention to the methodical pilot, Immelmann, who did not merely execute the orders given to him, but also took every extra opportunity to fly and was untiring in his efforts to acquire the war experience he still lacked.

AFFECTION AND LOYALTY

The advancement given by Kastner to the young pilot, even in the first few weeks, brought the consequence that my brother felt himself indissolubly bound to the section and its leader. This feeling of solidarity found expression in several touching little episodes:

The Flying Sections on the Western Front were supplied with the new Fokker Scouts in May, 1915, by Fokker himself, on the following system: the old, experienced war pilots were trained to fly the new machines on the aerodromes of their sections, but young pilots had to attend the Fokker School at Schwerin. Fokker visited Flying Section 62 in June, 1915; when in the course of the next few weeks my brother had to stand with others and watch him flying with Boelcke in the pupils' machine, he recognised the possibilities of this new invention. Then the desire to fly one of these nimble little birds must have become an overwhelming one, but since as a young pilot he would have been compelled to go to the school at Schwerin and thus leave the section and its leader, he refrained from making any application.

But my brother's renunciation met with its reward five months later when his captain allowed him to take off in a Fokker after one instructional flight with Boelcke, with the sensational and unique result that on the following day his tenacity and flying ability enabled him to shoot down one of three Englishmen whom he encountered.

A subsequent letter written by my brother also gives similar and stronger proof of the way in which the leader was conscious of this bond of solidarity, for in it he states that Captain Kastner was resolved to give up flying altogether 'if Immelmann was transferred from his section'.

The membership of a Flying Section was subject to continuous changes. But my brother was the static pole of Section 17, for after ten months at the front he was the only member of it who had gone out with Captain Kastner on May 13th, 1915. On June 13th, 1916, how ever, the hour struck for his departure from his beloved 62, which had become a new home to him and the last one he was to know. The section then went to the Eastern Front, leaving my brother behind in Douai as leader of an independent scouting formation. This promotion also brought about the parting from his leader, Captain Kastner.

Despite the differences in rank and age, the months of common experiences at the front which represented a phase of life so rich in successful labours led to the deep intimacy between the two men, of which the following letter, written by Captain Kastner to my mother, gives such touching proof:

"July 19th, 1916.

Dear Madam,

If after four weeks I can at length sum up courage to write to you, I shall certainly make no effort to offer consolations for a loss, the magnitude of which I can scarcely realise from the standpoint of our country or of aviation and shall never be able to even guess from a mother's standpoint.

My delay in writing before must also be ascribed to the events of war, which have brought such surprising changes to our old 62 and particularly to myself during the last days.

I do not know, Madam, whether your son ever told you of the relations existing between us or of the pride I took in him and the happiness I experienced in being witness of his glorious career. The grief I feel for his heroic death could not be greater or more genuine if I had lost my best friend, and it has also perhaps prevented me from using words which can never reproduce my real feelings.

I felt strangely moved when on the evening of June 14th I parted from the jewel of my section who has brought me so much joy and honour, from the 'little lad', as I called him on account of his youthful vigour and energy, which were coupled with a truly childish temperament. It may have been some foreboding which made the parting particularly hard for him, while I likewise could not resist the impression that I was compelled to leave the glory and the best of my section behind me.

Since our parting no day has passed or can pass without my thinking of him or telling my corps of officers, which is six times as large as Section 62, of his life and holding him up as the airman who achieved such incredible deeds and opened up new possibilities for aviation by his loyalty and devotion. In this way he still lives on among us, and for our human intelligence the only possible consolation is the fact that he won this true immortality by his creative achievements, i.e. in performing deeds which no one had hitherto performed. The photographs of himself which he gave me and the many souvenirs of him which came to me in the old section now constitute my most precious treasures, in which I can take delight when I am alone in my room, thinking of

those unforgettable hours I passed with him when we discussed service affairs, non-service affairs, human affairs and
affairs that were all too human. Often I had the feeling that
I was permitted to educate a younger brother. In this way I
lived and worked with your son; I do not know, but I hope
that he had similar thoughts of me. You may therefore be
assured, Madam, that under these circumstances I sympa-
thise with you as far as it is humanly possible to do.

Please remember me to your daughter, to whom I also
express my deepest sympathy.

Yours sincerely,
Kastner."

THE FORMATION OF FLYING SECTION 62

"Berlin, May 6th, 1915.
My sojourn with Section 10 in Vrizy was not a long one.
Telegraphic orders came to us at the end of April: 'Section to
send a biplane pilot to Döberitz at once.'

I reached Döberitz on April 28th and learnt that I was to
join a new section which was being raised to fly L.V.G.
biplanes, and that this section would be No. 62, its leader
being Captain Kastner, a man who had already made a name
for himself by numerous pre-war flights.

Of the six pilots, two are officers, Lieutenant Franceson
and Lieutenant Boelcke, and then there are three lance-cor-
porals. Among the observers there is one old airman,
Captain Ritter, with an artilleryman, a dragoon, a hussar, a
guard hussar and finally Lieutenant von Teubern, with
whom I was in the cadet corps.

On May 5th we were all ready. The machines were serviceable, the motor transport complete and the men up to strength. We expect to be ordered to the front any day."

THE YOUTHFUL GERMAN AIR ARM: A SURVEY

Since we have now reached the period when my brother's activities at the front commence, it would seem appropriate to make a survey of the events of the war in general and the development of war flying in particular in order to induce a clear understanding of the contents of his letters.

When he left for the front, it was at the time when Joffre was making his third attempt—with the reinforcements of the 1915 class which had been trained the previous winter—to break the iron grip of the Germans by means of a mighty offensive. This offensive is known as the Battle of Arras and La Bassée. The enemy's immediate objectives were the Lorette heights, the Souchez sugar factory, which was the scene of so much hot fighting and most especially the railway lines behind the German front, with their junctions at Lille, Douai and Vouziers.

Flying Section 62 was ordered into this focus point of military operations on the Western Front and given an aerodrome at Douai.

As regards the war in the air, the situation was almost as unfavourable for the German airmen as it was in the Winter Battle of the Champagne, i.e., the enemy was practically supreme in the air over the battle area.

Although the reacquisition of aerial supremacy was essentially due to the achievements of Boelcke, my brother and other warlike German airmen, it may also be ascribed in some measure to the development of German military aviation, which received an upward impetus at this very moment, because the Higher Command had at last begun to learn from its great sins of omission.

The cause of the German aerial inferiority which was undoubtedly manifested at the beginning of trench warfare is due to the different developments undergone by French and German pre-war aviation.

THE DEVELOPMENT OF THE AIR ARM

The extraordinarily good progress made in the construction of our airships—Zeppelin, Parseval, etc.—led our military authorities to an over-estimation of the airship for purposes of war, which was coupled with an under-estimation of the aeroplane, with the result that the outbreak of war found the German military aviation scarcely past its teething troubles. In France, however, developments proceeded in an exactly opposite direction, and consequently that country entered the war with a well-organised flying corps, so that the German aeroplanes on the Western Front found themselves opposed by 600 allied machines.

Although the surprisingly excellent reconnaissance results achieved by the German airmen during the forward movement opened the eyes of the Higher Command to the value of a good, strong aviation corps, a deep-seated cleavage in the authority over the aircraft units rendered impossible the energetic organisatory measures which was the only guarantee of any improvement in the fighting power of the air forces. Not until the Higher Command had learnt the lessons of the Winter Battle of the Champagne, in which the army commanders were obliged practically to dispense with

aerial reconnaissances on account of the German aerial inferiority—to the great disadvantage of the ground forces—
were measures taken to separate the youthful air arm from
the group of transport units (railwaymen, motor transport,
etc.) and put it under the command of a single individual in
March, 1915. This command was entrusted to Major
Thomsen, of the General Staff, who assumed the title of
'Chief of War Aviation'.

Within the limitations prescribed for him by the cliquish-
ness which flourished gaily despite the bitter events of the
war, this far-sighted, energetic man, who had already recognised in pre-war days the significance of the aerial arm in
any future warfare, succeeded in creating a vigorous organisation for the air forces and eliminating the existing defects.
Despite the marked German numerical inferiority this suf-
ficed to ensure the Higher Command the aerial supremacy in
the main battle areas of that period.

In addition to his new measures dealing with the organisation of the aircraft units and the creation of a central
authority for the same in the person of an Aviation Staff
Officer the 'Chief of War Aviation' promptly undertook the
very urgent task of arming the aircraft for offensive purposes.

Although both the French and German machines entered
the war unarmed, France experimented extensively with
aeroplane armaments in pre-war years, with the result that
the completely defenceless German airmen encountered
opponents equipped with machine guns as soon as trench
warfare started. During the Winter Battle of the Champagne
our unarmed machines were exposed to attacks by the very
speedy French 'avions de chasse', which possessed high
manœuvreability. The slow, clumsy, unarmed German recon-

naissance (B.) machines proved easy victims to these light one-seater scouts (Morane-Saulnier Parasol, Nieuport, etc.) which were equipped with forward pivotable or rigid machine guns. Individual French scout-fliers, such as Garros Guynemer, Dorme and Navarre, were able to make names for themselves with practically no attendant risks when flying these machines, for they shot down a number of German airmen or forced them to land. Above all, they caused considerable interruption to our tactical reconnaissance work, which they sometimes held up completely for a period.

The superior development of French war aviation brought other consequences, for the French Higher Command did not limit its use of the air arm to tactical operations (reconnaissance of enemy positions, direction of artillery fire, etc.), as the German Higher Command did, but also employed it for offensive work (bomb raids on Cologne, Friedrichshafen, Freiburg i B. and Düsseldorf), with at least an excellent moral effect. The defensive weapons employed by the Germans against the raiders were mainly anti-balloon or anti-aircraft batteries, which proved completely inadequate, because it was only by pure chance that they could score any hits.

Finally, about the commencement of 1916 the French began to develop a definite aerial strategy by sending up groups of three or four scout machines, working under leaders, to attack the individual German machines.

Nearly three months elapsed before my brother initiated these close-formation flights for the Germans with his group of single-seater fighters. After his death these methods were further developed by Boelcke and extended and perfected in masterly fashion by Richthofen.

Consequently the armament of aircraft was a more than

urgent problem which confronted the Chief of War Aviation in March, 1915. He made energetic demands on the immature German aircraft industry for the creation of three new types of machines. The results were:

I. THE C MACHINE

The seating arrangements were altered so as to bring the pilot in front and place him immediately behind the engine, with h.p. which had been increased from 80-160. The back seat occupied by the observer, who was equipped with a pivotable machine gun, gave him the necessary unimpeded view of the space behind, above and below him.

The C machine was employed on long distance reconnaissances and escort duties; the airmen of those days termed it the 'fighter machine'. Its crews were no longer defenceless when they took off on reconnaissance flights which often carried them a long way into the enemy's territory; moreover, the unarmed B type of machine could be protected by C fliers on close reconnaissances and artillery direction work, which sometimes lasted for several hours on end. At that period the C machine was also used to repel and attack enemy bombers, where fore the two fighting squadrons, stationed at Metz and Ostende, were equipped entirely with these machines.

Our pugnaciously disposed airmen could then accept any combats offered to them when out on escort or reconnaissance duty with the feeling that they were at least equal in armament to their opponents. By reason of the numerous victories they obtained they succeeded in at least restoring the aerial balance of power in a surprisingly short time.

Flying Section 62 also received a C machine at the end of May. As my brother writes, it was 'naturally assigned to our senior and best pilot, Boelcke'. A month later, when this C machine was acting as escort to an artillery flier, its observer, Lieutenant von Wühlisch—assisted by the skilful flying of his pilot, Boelcke—succeeded in shooting down an enemy machine. The German aircraft industry also evolved:

II. THE G MACHINE

Destined originally by the Chief of War Aviation for use as a bomber and equipped with two engines and two pivotable machine guns, this type was supplied to the fighting squadrons in place of their C machines. But instead of performing its valuable function of bombing, it was used by the fighting squadrons—probably on account of the excellent fighting power furnished by the effective fire of its two guns—for the same purposes as its C predecessor, i.e., for barrage patrols and the protection of captive balloons. It was, however, unable to fulfil these tasks, because, despite an effective range of fire, its clumsiness supplied many victims to the nimble French scouts. Then, in course of time, it came to be applied to its proper purpose and did excellent service as a night-bomber.

The best result achieved by the aircraft industry was the creation of the third type of machine required:

III. THE E MACHINE

This small one-seater fighter (Fokker), produced in the Fokker Works at Schwerin, provided the big surprise for our opponents. An 80 h.p. engine gave this monoplane—which weighed only 6 cwt.—a speed of 130 kilometres an hour, with a climbing capacity of about 3,500 metres (ceiling) in an hour. To these flying qualities, which were so amazing for 1915, were added great manœuvreability and an excellent armament. Some previous French armament experiments underwent a basic improvement, in that the rigid machine gun fired through the circle made by the propeller was equipped with an ingenious interrupter gear which prevented the emission of any bullets at the moments when one or other of the propeller blades passed in front of the barrel. This device rendered it theoretically impossible for any bullets to strike the propeller.

The most remarkable success achieved by our scouts on this type of machine—five victories for my brother and three for Boelcke—indicated the right direction for the further development of the scout machine, i.e., an increase in engine power and efficiency of fire without the addition of further weight. First the seven cylinder engine had its h.p. raised from 80-100 h.p., and then a second rigid machine gun was added. At the beginning of 1916 the h.p. was further increased to 160 by placing a second 80 h.p. engine behind the first and connecting the two.

As it was hardly possible to effect any radical alterations to the fuselage, this machine became practically a flying engine. As long as this engine, consisting of two star-shaped banks of seven cylinders, did its duty and rotated itself and its propeller 140 times a minute regularly round its axle, it imparted some unique flying qualities to the machine, to which it was attached by means of steel tubes. The slightest engine trouble and any consequent irregularity in the engine's revolutions made it necessary for the pilot to switch off his engine and abandon his flight, because the machine became virtually uncontrollable when the engine lost any of its efficiency.

Finally a third machine gun was added, and attempts were made to accelerate the rate of fire. As these developments which I have described naturally suffered from childish ailments, the first fighting pilots, who were also the first airmen to put the machines to practical test, suffered most from their initial shortcomings, while my brother had to pay with his life for this intensive development in one direction.

Both Boelcke and my brother often complained of engine trouble in their 160 h.p. Fokkers, and many a fight had to be broken off for this reason. But what made matters considerably worse was the fact that the interruptor gear did not always fulfil its functions faultlessly when the machine carried two or three guns.

Once in March, 1916, my brother sawed both his propeller blades cleanly off by shots from his own machine gun and was forced to make a hurried landing. Shortly afterwards the struts attaching the engine to the machine broke after one of Boelcke's flights, but he succeeded in landing safely. It was subsequently ascertained that he had shot off one blade of the propeller, whereupon the irregular revolutions of the engine caused the struts to break. In May the same thing happened to my brother again, but he also succeeded in landing safely. The same grave accident occurred again on June 18th, 1916, with disastrous results which caused the machine to break up in mid-air and occasioned my brother's death.

Shortly afterwards the system of the interruptor gear was changed, so that the gun was operated directly by the propeller. It was no longer loaded by the recoil, but by the turning movement of the propeller, which meant, in fact, that the engine's axle was utilised for this purpose. The result was that the rate of fire was doubled, and the effect was the same as that which would have been achieved by six machine guns. At the same time the rotary engine was replaced by a static one which could lose a propeller blade without serious consequences. Furthermore, the monoplane type gave way to a biplane.

These, however, were later developments which my brother did not live to see. In any case, none of the subsequent types of scout machines assumed such importance for Germany's aerial warfare as did the first German one-seater fighter, the 'Fokker E'.

When flown by fourteen experienced pilots (including Boelcke, Parschau, Althaus and Höhndorf) and a fifteenth in the person of the young pilot, Immelmann, who had not been long at the front, this Fokker E.1 achieved within the space of a few weeks—as is clearly shown from my brother's letters—an unlimited German aerial supremacy, which was maintained with better types of Fokkers until my brother's death.

How well this little machine, (which was so difficult to fly on account of its instability), suited my brother's flying skill is shown by the most incredible achievement of this young pilot who, although undergoing no training like the other Fokker pilots, took off to chase an enemy squadron on the third day with the machine, engaged in a fight with three Englishmen and brought down one of his opponents in his own methodical, tenacious fashion, having mastered all its difficulties, such as gun stoppages.

The complete familiarity with his Fokker E which he acquired in such a short time, had its disadvantages as well, because his opponents were enabled to recognise him and deduce the consequences of an encounter.

As the one-seater's rigid machine gun made it necessary for the pilot to aim with his machine and did not permit him to fire in any direction except straight ahead, leaving him therefore defenceless against an attack from the rear, my brother was not long in realising that it was impossible to lay down any definite rules for fighting in a Fokker, especially if it was attacking another machine. But his extraordinary composure and tenacity, combined with a will to give of his best, enabled him to deduce in scientific fashion from innumerable air combats the best means of attack to be employed against every enemy type of machine. The methods which he was the first to apply in airfights and the flying manœuvres associated with them are standards for the training of all post-war scouting and stunting pilots. Even today the movement known as the 'Immelmann turn', which was first practised by my brother, is demonstrated at flying displays. This consists of a short climb in combination with a half-roll, and evidently my brother's experience of aerial combats showed him that this was the best method of attacking a certain English type of biplane since it reduced the risks to a minimum because the enemy observer was unable to shoot on account of the obstruction presented by his own steering surfaces.

Almost every day my brother sent the Aviation Staff Officer of the 6th Army reports based on his experiences of aerial warfare, and the deductions they drew from them were made public in the form of advice and definite instructions to the other fighting pilots.

If by the end of 1916 we find the Jagdstaffels always flying in formation for front patrols, it must be remembered that an attack on an enemy formation always broke up the mass encounter into a series of single combats, just as it did when scout flying started. In these 'dog-fights' the rules for attacking an opponent as well as for completing or breaking off the fight remained unaltered from the time when they were first applied and defined by my brother. Thus they finally became common property of all German scouts.

My brother also seems to have divined the further developments of aerial warfare, because it is by no mere matter of chance that the establishment of a group of one-seater fighters, over which he was given command, first took place in the sector belonging to the army for which he worked.

As I have already remarked, the first Fokkers were allotted to the most experienced pilots, after which every flying section on the Western Front received at least one of these machines in the course of 1915. But this distribution of the Fokkers among the various sections attached to each army meant that considerable distances separated the Fokker pilots from one another. When an enemy formation was reported, it was therefore impossible for them to launch a concerted attack upon it.

Major Stempel, the Aviation Staff Officer of the 6th Army and a man who had done valuable work in the formation of the Bavarian flying corps in pre-war times, perceived this disadvantage. In order to eliminate it he took steps which were to prove of vital importance for the organic construction of future scout forces.

As early as 1915 he organised the Fokker pilots belonging to all the sections stationed at Douai into a 'fighting defence force' under the command of my brother, who thus became the first leader of a scout formation. Although this force (it was not long before two other similar ones were constituted) did not act as an independent unit, it may nevertheless be regarded as a preliminary step towards the creation of the later Jagdstaffels.

This grouping of Fokker pilots was shown to be so practical that on June 10th, 1916, my brother received orders to raise the first independent fighter Staffel which should take its orders direct from the Army H.Q. Unfortunately his death-flight a week later prevented him from carrying out this task.

It is furthermore to be regretted that the formation of this fighting Staffel was abandoned on account of his death. The creation of fighting Staffels was therefore not achieved until August, 1916, to the great detriment of German military operations in the meanwhile, because the commencement of the Battle of the Somme saw our solitary scouts and reconnaissance fliers faced by numerous strong and well organised enemy formations, who won the supremacy of the air in a very short time and debarred our airmen from any view of the fighting area. Our infantry and artillery were therefore left without any protection when exposed to the massed fire of enemy artillery, because the lack of information from the air made it impossible for our own batteries to take effective counter-measures.

Thus the absence of my brother and the consequent absence of Boelcke, who was sent on leave until the end of August on account of his death, resulted in the loss within a few weeks of the-aerial supremacy which had been maintained up to that time. And it is this fact which shows perhaps more than any other one the marked importance of our first German scout-fliers and the unbreakable link that unites the development of scout flying and the history of aerial warfare with the first appearance of the Fokker E.

machine and the name of Immelmann, who was its most successful pilot. His letters, which I shall reproduce in subsequent chapters—'the sober accounts of an enthusiastic airman', as he terms them—give a clear picture of the evolution of German war flying and provide him with a better monument than any sculptor could fashion.

RECONNAISSANCES ON THE SOMME

"Douai, May 27th, 1915.
We left Döberitz a fortnight ago. Today, at last, I can tell you all the details of the last few weeks, or such of them that I did not tell you in Dresden.

The new section was ready on May 5th. The machines were serviceable. The motor transport was complete, and the men were up to strength. From day to day we awaited our orders for the front. At last, on May 13th, Ascension Day, we started off, but no one knew whither. Our departure was quite nice; the cars, the machines and we ourselves were decorated with flowers and greenery.

It is much pleasanter to go to the front with a new section than to be drafted into an old, war-experienced one as a novice. You feel that you really belong to the section when you have experienced its formation, its early stages and its growth. But I cannot complain of my welcome from No. 10.

We were well looked after during the three days of our journey, and we reached Pont Faverger, our destination, on the Saturday. We detrained our machines and motor transport very quickly and stowed everything away in the sheds built by our predecessors, No. 13. Then I sought out my billet, which was quite decent.

The next day we assembled the machines, i.e. refitted them with the wings and steering surfaces which had been dismantled for the journey. My machine was ready first. After a short trial flight which was to show me whether it was properly braced, I flew off to Rethel, where I had left my flying kit, bedding, etc., stowed away. I was back again in the evening.

My batman had just finished putting my room straight when orders came for the section to stand by for a remove to Douai. So the following morning we packed up again, dismantled the machines and put everything on the train, so that we were ready to start at 2 p.m. We left Pont Faverger with mixed feelings, because it was a nice village. Certainly, however, we had little hope of anything much in the way of war or flying there. We expected things to be different in Douai, because we knew the French were going to try to break through at Arras.

We arrived after an eight hour journey, but were held up outside Douai for fully twenty-four hours because the sidings were taken up by other trains. When this wait was over, we detrained quickly and drove off to the aerodrome, which is 4 kilometres outside Douai. It is a pre-war aerodrome.

Our tents were soon pitched. My tent was ready first, as was fit and proper. On returning to the town, I did not find my billet until late in the evening, after much wandering. I was quartered on an old woman, and found everything terribly dirty.

Douai is quite a small town, about the size of Stendal, I judge, and only as comparatively dirtier as a French town would be. At present there are a lot of soldiers there, which is the reason why we found only moderately good billets. We made efforts to secure better quarters and also a mess, for which purpose Lieutenant von Teubern, Lieutenant

Boelcke and I went off on a search.

Our efforts were successful, for we found a small house that afforded perfect quarters for two officers. It was an empty villa. We fetched the keys, and lo! there was a small mess for us, consisting of writing-room, smoking-room and dining-room. On the first floor there were two large rooms and a bathroom, on the second a large room and two small ones. I annexed the large one, so that I now have excellent accommodation.

Our machine trials the next morning were soon over, and then we were free. We three went into the town together— von Teubern (observer), Boelcke (pilot) and myself. It soon transpired that we suit one another very well. None of us smoke, and we practically never touch alcohol, but we are very fond of cakes. I knew von Teubern some years ago in the cadet corps. Boelcke is an accomplished sportsman in the most varied directions. He is an extraordinarily quiet, reflective fellow with sensible views, and he owes it to his mode of life that he doesn't show the slightest sign of life, although he has been flying since the beginning of the war and spent quite a long time at the front with No. 13. He flies finely and has the First Class of the Iron Cross.

Our war flying was to begin the following day. I was ordered to fly with von Teubern. We got up at 5 a.m., and were ready to take off at 6. But for two days we turned up at the aerodrome in vain, because it rained all the time. On the third St. Peter was kind to us.

Flying Section 20, which has been here some time, told us some horrible tales. It is impossible to cross the French lines, they say, because the French artillery shoots so well. Moreover all the French machines are equipped with machine guns, which in itself is a reason why one cannot cross the lines. I was the first in the section to go up, and when I returned, I learnt I was the only one.

Being a cautious man, I climbed up to 2,700 metres on the strength of these warnings and was prepared for the worst. The enemy's artillery was lively and did not shoot badly. We did our job in spite of the efforts of an enemy plane to close with us. On our return we were welcomed with great joy by the section as the men who had broken the ice for them.

I have now done seven flights altogether here, some of them with quite nice success. Sometimes I go up with von Teubern and sometimes with my proper observer, Captain Ritter. Our main tasks are to photograph the enemy's positions and reconnoitre his movements. Our sector comprises such well-known places as Arras, Neuve Chapelle, Neuveville, Givenchy and Souchez. Flying is quite lively here and quite in accordance with the activities of the front.

Several days ago two French machines were shot down here, and the day before yesterday French aircraft dropped 28 bombs on our aerodrome, without hitting anything. Yesterday one of our machines was attacked by three enemy ones, and after several shots it was forced to land, although the inmates did not know where they were. Their joy was naturally great when they came down somewhere to the east of Ypres and therefore in our territory. The machine was completely smashed up when it landed, the pilot came down in some trenches which our men captured from the English only a few weeks before.

The French and English have been trying for several weeks to break through between Arras and Souchez, but they have not succeeded, and never will. They may take a few trenches, but only with enormous losses. If they use coloured troops, they will not be able to hold them. The big Winter Battle of the Champagne was just the same, because they bought a few hundred metres of ground there with most incredible losses.

There's no harm in Italy having come in. The abandonment of the attack on the Dardanelles, the investment of Prczymisl, or whatever you call the place, the chancellor's speech and the Lusitania Note make very joyful news."

THE FIRST AIRFIGHT

"Douai, June 3rd, 1915.
Although I sent you off a long letter only yesterday, I am nevertheless writing to you again today. I encountered my first troubles when I flew yesterday and today. Lieutenant von Teubern was my observer both times. We climbed up to 2,500 metres and made our first attempt to cross the lines over Arras. There an enemy aeroplane, armed with a machine gun, came flying towards us. I therefore turned and flew northwards towards Lens, in order to cross the lines there, but another enemy came to meet me. I flew on and headed straight for him. When the enemy aircraft saw I was flying on, he probably feared I might have a machine gun on board, and so he turned round and flew back. Thereupon I veered round into the direction required by my job. As soon as the enemy saw this, he made for me again. Then I went for him once more, and he promptly turned back. This nice little game was repeated until we had carried out our task, which was to photograph certain enemy positions, after which we were able to fly home unmolested.

The next day we had a similar job. We flew over the positions, and Lieutenant von Teubern photographed them. In the distance I saw an enemy aircraft, a Farman biplane, making for us. He seemed to be about 200 metres higher than our machine.

He came nearer and nearer and finally became invisible when he was vertically above us, because the wings block our direct upward view. Suddenly I heard the familiar tack-tack-tack-tack of the machine guns and saw little holes appear in our right wing. After about ten shots there was a short pause. Meanwhile von Teubern had made six exposures, but wanted to go on photographing.

Now the shooting starts again. Suddenly I hear the bullets striking something metallic. If the brute shoots up my engine, there is nothing more to be done! At last Teubern is finished. It is a horrible feeling to have to wait until one is perhaps hit, without being able to fire a shot oneself! Again I hear a noise like someone drumming on a metal plate.

At last Teubern is finished. Now we hurriedly drop 200 metres and head straight for Douai, where I land uninjured on our aerodrome.

When we landed, they counted our bullet-holes. There are about five or six harmless ones in the wings. A solitary one grazed our main spar, without breaking it. One shot went clean through the engine's bed. The metal cowling which encloses the lower part of the engine looks like a sieve. My machine is the first here to have been so knocked about by enemy fire. We are glad we got down so well that time.

So now I have experienced something at last. But I have not merely experienced something; I have also gained something, for today our captain handed me the Second Class of the Iron Cross, with some words of appreciation.

That is all I can tell you today."

TO ARMS!

"Douai, June 25th, 1915.
This time I do not need to apologise for my failure to write. No matter how diligent I had been with my letters, they would not have gone off, because the post has been suspended. As far as I know, the ban has not yet been lifted, but I shall use the rainy day to write. I will start by answering your questions.

Certainly this was and is one of the most difficult areas from the airman's point of view, because the French have collected all sorts of means of defence against aircraft. That was why Section 20, who have been here seven months, told us it was impossible to fly across the lines. Teubern and I were the first of our section to prove that it was possible. In that way we have broken the ice (or the prejudice) for the section. Now our airmen think nothing of flying 25-30 kilometres behind the French lines. We could see that as a matter of fact Section 20 did not do much flying. We have made a lot of flights; in our section I have the most (21) to my name, and then comes Lieutenant Boelcke with 19. But he did 60 70 with Section 13 before he came to us.

As you will have read in the paper, an enemy machine was forced to land near Douai. Our captain went off there and saw it carried a machine gun. He asked the authorities who are in charge of the spoils if he might have it, and he got it. Then this captured French machine gun was mounted in our speediest and best climbing machine, a small so-called L.V.G., under our captain's directions.

Lieutenant Boelcke flew this little L.V.G., which does about 120 kilometres an hour, climbs to about 2,000 metres in 20–22 minutes and can get up to 3,200–3,300 in an hour.

The normal L.V.G. cannot reach 2,000 in under 40 minutes and takes an hour to get up to 2,200–2,300.

Then one day a proper fighting machine arrived, i.e. a machine with a 150 h.p. engine, which was built by the factory as a fighting machine and armed with a machine gun. Naturally our senior and best pilot, Lieutenant Boelcke, got it, while the 'auxiliary' fighter with the captured French machine gun which he had been using went to the next best, and that was me. So now I have the little L.V.G., which can climb and fly much faster but is also somewhat more difficult to handle. I took this bus up to 3,200 on the very first day, and climbed to 3,500 several days afterwards.

The next thing I did was to have the machine gun remounted where I thought best. We made such a good job of it that not merely was everyone pleased, but the captain ordered a photograph to be taken and sent to the aviation staff officer as an example of a particularly good mounting of a captured machine gun. I am sending you the snaps in this letter. The roller is a drum, on which is wound a steel belt with a hundred cartridges. These hundred shots can be fired in ten seconds.

Although my 'auxiliary fighter' is only a makeshift, at least my observer can rattle away with his gun, and that makes a permanent impression on the French airmen.

I have already made several flights in the new machine. We had an airfight on our second flight, and it ended with a forced landing for us. The enemy had a machine gun too, and put a bullet in our petrol tank. All the petrol ran out in a moment, and I had to make a quick landing. I have kept the bullet; it is a French copper one, and along its side you can see the impressions made by the barrel. Its point must have slid along the sheet-brass of our tank, because it

Max Immelmann, Oberleutnant.

Original World War I postcard titled,
"Our Flying Hero Oberleutnant Immelmann."

Immelmann as an acrobat in the Cadet Display of 1910.

Immelmann (x) as Senior of his room in the Cadet Corps,
Dresden, 1910.

Immelmann (x) as an ensign in the 2nd Railway Regiment.

Immelmann in the Harz Mountains Winter Trials, 1913.

Immelmann as an aviation pupil in an L.V.G.

Immelmann with Lieut. von Teuben, after his first air fight.

Immelmann in a 150 h.p. L.V.G biplane (C. model).

Immelmann in the first German scout craft, the 80 h.p.
Fokker E.1.

A steep "corkscrew" in an L.V.G.

Protecting an L.V.G. in a Fokker.

The pilot's seat in the 80 h.p. Fokker.

*The 14-cylinder rotary engine and the three machine guns of the
160 h.p. Fokker.*

Immelman's 25th birthday. A photograph taken at the scene of the wreckage of his third victim.

Victory No. 4. A Bristol biplane shot down near Berlingham.

No. 7. A Morane-Saulnier shot down near Valenciennes.

The King of Saxony (x) visits Flying Section 24 at Lille and presents Immelmann (xx) with a Meissen porcelain plate.

Österreicher, Boelcke and Immelmann at lunch in the starting hut on Douai aerodrome.

On leave in Leipzig with his mother.

Flying Section 62, January 20th, 1916, with the two "Pour le Mérite" airmen, Boelcke and Immelmann.

The wreckage of No. 11, a Bristol biplane shot down near Moncy.

Immelmann with Crown Prince Boris of Bulgaria.

No. 13, a Bristol biplane.

A visit of neutral officers to Flying Section 62, May 31st, 1916.

The dead airman's homeward journey. Immelman's funeral procession in Douai.

The last resting place of the Eagle of Lille,
in the Grove of Urns in Dresden.

is flattened and coated over with brass.

We were luckier on another flight, when we succeeded in forcing two enemy aircraft to retreat. We cannot tell whether they were hit. As we have only the two fighters, I have now considerably more to do, because we have to escort the other machines which are unarmed.

We have just got two small one-seater fighters from the Fokker factory. The crown prince of Bavaria visited our aerodrome to see these new fighting machines and inspected us and Section 20. Director Fokker, the constructor of this fighter, was presented to him. Fokker and a Lieutenant Parschau gave exhibition flights for him and fired at ground targets from the air. Fokker amazed us with his ability.

When we heard of the capture of Lemberg, on the eastern front, all the bells were pealed from 10-11 p.m. It gives one a strange feeling to hear the French bells of occupied territory pealing for a German victory.

That is all the news."

PROGRESS AND SUCCESS

"Douai, July 17th, 1915.
Once again I have a whole lot of things to tell. It is quite a long time since I last wrote to you.

I told you in my last letter that Director Fokker demonstrated one of the one-seater fighters built in his factory. He is one of the oldest and best airmen. I am very much in his good books, not only for my flying, but for my mode of life as well, because I do not smoke or drink, and always go to bed early. I never stay in the mess after 10 p.m.

One day Fokker learnt that I am an engineer and not a regular soldier. The next day he asked me whether I would like to go into his factory after the war, starting as his chief pilot and taking an engineer's job as soon as I had acquired the necessary knowledge. He said he needed men like me, but that they were difficult to find!

We have fixed it all up. I should get a regular salary and a percentage on all machines taken over from me and on all pupils I trained. He guaranteed (in the presence of witnesses) to give me a job after the war, but I am in no way bound to him. If I don't want to go, the whole thing is off.

Isn't that a fine reward for a respectable life? I am glad to have something tangible in case I need it after the war. Fokker went away several days ago, but left a one-seater fighter behind. Naturally, Lieutenant Boelcke is to fly it.

These little craft absorb my entire interest. They are pretty machines, and they are light, speedy and nimble. The pilot flies alone. He operates the machine gun himself; it is fired through the circle of the propeller. The machine is designed solely for fighting enemy airmen, and not for reconnaissance work.

I have got the 150 h.p. biplane fighter which became vacant when Lieutenant Boelcke took the one-seater fighter. As a junior pilot I can be very satisfied with it, because it means progress for me. With this fighter, which is one of the so-called C machines, one can cross the lines and see an enemy machine approach without suffering from that feeling of definite inferiority which undoubtedly attacks anyone in one of the other machines without a machine gun. In the machines I flew previously a speedy retreat was the best means of defence against enemy airmen. Things are going to be different now.

The machine has been tested in action, because several days ago Lieutenants Boelcke (pilot) and von Wühlisch (observer) brought down a French Parasol machine when flying it. There was great rejoicing in the section! Von Wühlisch got the First Class of the Iron Cross; Boelcke has it already.

I can assert without exaggeration that Section 62 has put some life into the Douai flying. We have made a good start here, as may be seen firstly from the praise given us by Prince Heinrich but, above all, because our leader always does everything that has to be done for the general good.

In our neighbourhood there is a section which has still to fly the old 100 h.p. L.V.G.'s. They haven't got a single modern machine. But we have bettered ourselves in the meanwhile! We went to the front with six big old L.V.G.'s, but while there are sections which have been out for 5-10 months without getting a fighting machine, we were given a 150 h.p. L.V.G. fighter when we had been four weeks at the front. Meanwhile another L.V.G. fighter is on its way to us, so that now we have only one of the old machines left.

We can therefore say that the section has come on splendidly. Personally, I, too, can be very satisfied at having been given a fighter when I am still such a junior pilot. When I told an acquaintance in Lille, who is also an airman, that I was flying a 150 h.p. fighter, he asked me with great amazement: 'Are you the senior pilot in your section?'

That I am certainly not. Of the nine pilots in our section six are older than me, and only two younger. (I mean in flying age.)

LOST!

Last Monday I had an experience which could have been very unpleasant, but finally turned out quite well.

After my 150 h.p. L.V.G. had undergone some repairs, I
wanted to try it out, in order to see whether the petrol pipe
was working properly, because it had failed me at a great
height. The sky was fairly cloudy, and there was a strong
west wind. I climbed higher and higher. After an hour's flying I was up to 3,700, the greatest height I had ever reached
so far. When I looked down, I couldn't see a sign of the
ground; there was a thick cloudbank about 1,000 metres
below me.

During my climb I had paid no attention to the gathering
clouds. I had taken off without my observer, and was merely carrying a mechanic as ballast. Where was I?

I circled round for half an hour in the hope of seeing the
clouds break, but in vain. Finally I decided to push my way
through the clouds, and when I got below them, I was still
1,200 metres up. The country below me was completely
unfamiliar. I tried to locate it by my map, but without success. As I could see nothing unusual below, I decided to land
in order to find out where I was, and looked about for a suitable field.

Below me on my right there was a huge wood, covering
an area of many kilometres. To my left there was a wide
stretch of open ground, which seemed to be planted with
potatoes or turnips. I put the machine into a glide, but when
I dropped down to 500 metres, I received some lively
artillery fire. I switched on again and climbed as quickly as
possible; thus I escaped miraculously with a few holes in my
wings.

By reason of the aforesaid unfriendly welcome I was definitely convinced that I must be over enemy territory. But
wherever I was, the German country was bound to lie eastward. I climbed and soon rose above the clouds. A snow-

storm took me by surprise at 2,500 metres, so that for some while I could not see a thing.

I flew on, keeping the sun on my right. After an hour's flight I found the clouds dividing. A charming landscape lay below me. I glided down to 1,200 metres, but in spite of my height the ground seemed very close. The country was rather like the Harz mountains. The mountains must have been fairly high, because my altimetre still showed a height of 1,000 metres, and yet the ground was so very near. Soon I recognised by the type of the houses and the fencing of the fields, in short, by the general character of the landscape, that I must be in Belgium. The next thing was to find a landing place.

It was certainly no easy matter in those parts. Four times I flattened out to land, but each time, when I was from 5 to 10 metres off the ground, I saw that the meadow I had chosen was intersected by ditches and other obstacles. At last I found a barren hilltop which was meadowland hedged in only at the foot and crest. The slope rose sharply from north to south, but I was forced to land in an east to west direction on account of the strong wind.

I was just hovering above the ground when the slope caused my left wheel to touch it and break off. Luckily my speed was reduced considerably by an upward slope; nevertheless, my tail went up, and the propeller splintered. Several splinters tore holes in the upper wing; the machine stood on its engine, and I was left hanging by my belt.

Before landing I called to my passenger: 'Look out! Hold tight; we're going to crash!' So he had time to prepare for the coming events, and all went off well. We got out to have a look at the damage. As a matter of fact, only the left wheel and the propeller were broken. The hill was much steeper than I first thought—at least as steep as our Loschwitz Weinberg is at the summer-house. According to the altimeter we were 850 metres higher than at Douai.

Having congratulated myself on my escape, I gave the machine over to some Landsturmers who had hurried up. Then we began our descent.

After receiving a kindly welcome from the officers of the company quartered there, I went to their office and wired my section: 'Just landed at Trooz, between Liège and Verviers. Dismantling machine and returning by train.'

When my captain received the wire, he is said to have remarked:

'Well, the bus is finished, for there's no place to land there!'

He knew the country from August of last year.

How did I manage to cover the stretch between Douai and Liège in an hour? I learnt later that at 2,500 metres we struck a 30 metres a second wind, which means 108 kilometres an hour. When you add my machine's speed to that, it is easy for me to do a stretch of more than 200 kilometres in an hour.

After lunch my thoughts turned again toward the machine, which I was forced to dismantle, because it was impossible to think of taking off from that difficult ground, even if I managed to get spare parts. Under my directions some unskilful hands dismantled the machine, which they then conveyed with the greatest difficulty along a bad and narrow road to the station. Twelve men carried the right wing and another twelve the left; eight men accompanied the fuselage, which was drawn by two horses, while a cart carried the rudder and elevator parts.

Meanwhile I had asked for the use of a railway truck, which I obtained after some difficulty. It was waiting for me when I reached the station at 9.30 p.m. with my bits and pieces, and we began to load up at once. They wanted to attach me to a goods train leaving for Lille at 3 a.m., which meant I shouldn't have got home till the following evening. In desperation I put it to the station commandant that I had to get back to Douai as quickly as possible, and finally I succeeded in getting myself hooked on to the mail train which went off at 10.27 p.m. I travelled straight through to Douai, telephoned my arrival to the section at 11 a.m., and was on the aerodrome again at noon with my machine.

I quickly collected a bunch of mechanics, who got to work like mad. They had to put another wheel on, fix a new propeller, put the wings on and brace them as well as patch a few holes. It was feverish work for twenty men.

At 2 p.m., i.e., two hours later, the bird was all fixed up, so that I could go to the captain and report myself back from Trooz. He was not in a particularly good temper and merely asked: 'What's happened to the machine ?'

I was glad I was able to reply: 'The machine is serviceable and in her tent."

Then his face cleared visibly. He congratulated me on the happy ending to my flight and added: 'If you had smashed the bus up, you'd have had to fly the oldest machine in the section.'

However, all remains as it was. The section had given me up for lost, and all were genuinely pleased to see me again. I had my sleep out in the afternoon, because it was not flying weather, and I was dead tired after spending the whole night looking after my machine on an open truck."

LONG DISTANCE RECONNAISSANCES

"Douai, July 31st, 1915.
It is not my fault that you have been so long without news of me, because the post was held up again. The suspension is lifted now.

You would like to know something about my activities since I have been flying the fighter biplane. They are three:

1. Long distance reconnaissances are the bulk of our work.
2. As far as possible we have to protect the unarmed machines when they do their jobs.
3. We have to do our best to interrupt the activities of the enemy machines.

This last heading comprises the so-called air barrage, i.e., we patrol the lines to stop enemy airmen having a look behind our positions. This activity of theirs is most remunerative if their reconnaissance flights enable the enemy to get a picture of what is happening on the ground.

Several days ago our artillery planned to make a 'fire-raid' on the enemy's lines, i.e., to concentrate a large number of shells on his positions at a definite time (5-7 p.m.). As it is easy to spot a firing battery, the enemy airmen naturally go up at once to locate it and report its position to their own artillery, so that the latter can shoot more accurately. In such cases we have the task of stopping the enemy machine from prying into our territory.

As a matter of fact, two airmen tried to have a look, but each time we pounced on them like a hawk, so that neither stayed longer than five minutes. They seem to have a holy respect for a German machine gun.

At that time we had a splendid opportunity to observe the effect of artillery fire. Often columns of smoke rising up to 500 metres showed us that one of the enemy's munitions dumps or something of the sort had blown up. It was a fine sight. The reward for our activities was not lacking, for in addition to the Second Class of the Iron Cross I received on July 15th the Friedrich Augustus silver medal 'for Gallantry in Face of the Enemy'.

The war will last a good while yet. We are already in a winter campaign, because lately there were 8 degrees of frost at 3,500 metres. The latest barograph papers also contain one that shows my record height of 4,000 metres.

The weather has been changeable all the time, alternating between fine and rain. My duties have consisted mainly of long distance reconnaissances, in the course of which we have flown as far as St. Pol when there have not been too many enemy airmen about. While we were flying to St. Pol, Bethune and La Bassée at 3,000 metres up last Thursday, such a thick fog came on that we could not see the ground. I dropped down to 50 metres to ascertain how deep it extended. As I found myself continually buzzing round chimneys and steeples, landing was impossible. Douai was completely in the fog, so we flew on to Lille and landed there. Not until 11 a.m.—we took off at 5 a.m.—did it clear up sufficiently to let us get home.

Arras was on fire again yesterday. Several days ago a huge blaze was raging there. The smoke and steam rose up to 800 metres and then floated across to Douai. Not much of the cathedral is left. We can now consider the so-called Battle of Arras as over.

It is impossible for me to answer with definite figures your question about the heights at which we fly, because the height always depends on the job. If we want to photograph, we stick at 2,000-2,200 metres. If we are doing a long-distance reconnaissance, we generally climb to 2,800-3,000. We carry out our barrage patrols at 3,500-3,700 metres, or even higher, and climb to such heights because they make it easier for us to catch sight of the enemy and pounce on him. Besides, it is easier and more comfortable to shoot downwards than upwards. Some time ago Lieutenants Boelcke (pilot) and Wühlisch (observer) brought a Frenchman down by using these tactics, and yesterday a fighter forced an English machine to land in similar fashion.

In answer to your other questions, Bapaume is not in our sector, and I flew due east on my flight to Verviers.

So Franz is in the Vosges? There's a bit more going on there now. Yes, the foot artillery have to handle these terribly heavy guns, which is certainly a horrible business, but let us hope they get no worse experiences in the war.

I have been flying a lot again. I do the most flights in the section. So far our section has sustained no losses in any of its airfights.

Just one more tale to finish up, and then I think I have told you everything that has happened of late:

Our captain's birthday was on the 20th. There was a bit of a celebration in the mess. I cleared off early, as usual. When I had put my little dog to bed, I thought to myself: 'Really, you ought to have stopped a bit longer in the mess today in honour of the birthday child.' So I went back, and when I arrived, I was welcomed with loud 'hallos'. The noise grew worse, and finally several officers carried me up and down through the room on their shoulders.

At first I thought everyone was tight, but finally the cause of their joy was revealed. During my absence a telegram arrived: 'Ensign Immelmann promoted to lieutenant as from July 14th, 1915.' Great was then my joy, and I stayed in the mess until 2 a.m. to celebrate the day."

THE FIRST SCOUTING FLIGHT AND THE FIRST VICTORY

"Douai, August 3rd, 1915.
I have already written to you about the visit paid to us by Fokker, the director of the Fokker Works, which supply so many one-seater fighters to the army. At that time I had a great desire to learn to fly one of those fast light monoplanes, but I should have had to be posted to his flying school at Schwerin, and I did not want that. Well, when he went away, he left a school machine, i.e. one without a machine gun, here.

On Friday, the 30th, I asked Boelcke to take me up in this bus, so that I could see how he handled the controls. After watching him, I asked him to step out, and then I made five solo landings—all of them quite perfect. All the men watching were surprised at the good landings, because the difference between an L.V.G. biplane and a Fokker monoplane is as great as that between summer and winter. The next day I had a trial in one of the two war machines; I whizzed about in the air for 20 minutes and fired off 30 shots at a ground target, but unfortunately only hit it twice. Altogether I felt very happy in that little bird.

On August 1st I was down to do a reconnaissance with my observer. The car was to come for us at 4 a.m., but it was called off because the weather was bad. So we were able to go on sleeping.

At 4.45 a.m. by French time (5.45 a.m. by German time) I was woken up by a terrible row. I hurried to the window, and then I saw the fun. About ten enemy machines were cruising over our aerodrome at 2,500–3,200 metres and dropping bombs all the time. With the anti-aircraft guns firing as well, there was a row bigger than any I had heard for a long time.

So the weather must be all right for flying. I tell someone to telephone for a car at once, dress and go to the mess for breakfast. On the way I meet Boelcke, who is off on his motor bike, because he means to go up in his monoplane and chase the enemy away. Ten minutes later I too start for the aerodrome. My observer says he considers it useless to go up, because the visibility is too bad. That riles me; as I am out there, I want at least to take off.

There were at least ten enemy machines in the air. In the distance we saw Boelcke in pursuit of another monoplane. Since I am not a lazy man, I got the other Fokker out of its shed and buzzed off. When I had climbed up to 2,000 metres, two of the enemy flew over me, at about 2,600. They were heading in the direction of Arras, and I in the opposite one. I was glad they didn't attack me, because I should have been defenceless against them when flying 600 metres lower.

I was up to 2,400 by the time I was almost over Douai, and then I saw two other opponents and Boelcke. They were 3,200 metres up; all three were heading for Arras. Then I flew towards Arras as well, hoping to be high enough to help Boelcke by the time I got there, for I heard the rattle of machine guns.

Suddenly I saw Boelcke go down in a steep dive. As I

learnt later, he had a bad gun stoppage, so that he could not fire another shot. I was about halfway between Douai and Arras when I caught sight of a third machine a long way ahead of me. I could not see whether it was an enemy or one of our own, but I flew towards him.

Then I saw him drop bombs on Vitry. It was plain that he must be an enemy. I climbed a bit and made for him. I was about 80–100 metres above him when 50 away. I saw the huge French markings quite clearly—blue, white and red rings. There was no longer any doubt about him.

The two others were now heading for me, and they were still high above me. So I had to act quickly. I dived on him like a hawk and fired my machine gun. For a moment I thought I was going to fly right in to him. I had a gun stoppage when I had fired about 60 shots; that was most unpleasant because I needed both hands to remove it, which meant that I had to go on flying without handling the controls. It was a new and strange experience for me, but I managed it. The same thing happened twice more in the course of the fight.

Meanwhile the enemy was making for Arras. I flew alongside of him and cut off his line of retreat by forcing him into a left-hand turn, which put his machine in the direction of Douai. In the course of these manœuvres we went down about 400 metres. In the intervals of firing I heard faintly the rattle of the machine guns of the other foemen who were above me. I tried to keep my machine vertically above my opponent's, because no biplane can shoot straight up. After firing 450–500 shots in the course of a fight which lasted about 8–10 minutes, I saw the enemy go down in a steep glide. I went after him. I could fire no more shots, because my machine gun failed me. When I saw him land, I went down beside him, climbed out and went up to him. There was no one in the neighbourhood, and I was unarmed. Would the inmates offer resistance? It was an unpleasant moment.

I called out when still some distance away: 'Prisonniers!' Then I saw for the first time that there was only one man in the cockpit. He held up his right hand as a sign that he would offer no resistance,

I went up to him. I shook hands and said: 'Bon jour, monsieur.' But he answered in English.

'Ah, you are an Englishman?'

'Yes.'

'You are my prisoner.'

'My arm is broken; you shot very well.'

Then I saw for the first time that his left arm was badly wounded. I helped him out of the machine, laid him on the grass, took his gloves off and cut away the sleeves of his leather coat, tunic and shirt. A bullet had gone through his forearm.

Cars were arriving from all directions, for they had been watching the fight in Douai. I sent someone off at once for a doctor. I received the most cordial congratulations from all sides.

Now at last I had time to inspect the enemy machine. My shooting was good. Two shots in the propeller, but none in the engine; three in the petrol tank, four or five in the fuselage and six in the wings, while all the instruments such as altimeter, anemometer and rev-counter were shot to pieces. Further bullets had hit several bracing wires and control-cables, the bomb rack and the left wheel—almost everything was shot to pieces. There were about 40 hits on the machine.

Having seen the captured machine placed under a military guard and the wounded man in the doctor's hands, I flew off home again. Then I returned to my captured machine by car, because our captain had gone off there in the meanwhile. He was vastly delighted and very proud; because it was the third enemy machine brought down by his section.

The wounded pilot, a young English lieutenant named William Reid, had meanwhile been taken to hospital.

On returning to the aerodrome once more, I took off again—this time in my 150 h.p. biplane, and dropped a note over St. Pol, telling them that we had brought one of their machines down.

In the mess I was the hero of the day. There was no jealousy in the congratulations of my comrades. Boelcke, who watched the fight from below, ran out on to the aerodrome and shouted: 'They will shoot our Immelmann dead!' But they did not shoot me dead. I was told that my turns and glides and my flying in general looked as if I had been in a Fokker for weeks instead of three days.

Yesterday I received the First Class of the Iron Cross as a mark of distinction. So now I have the nicest decoration any young officer can get. I have nothing against you letting it be known in the ordinary way that I have got the I.C.I, but you must in no case give anyone a photograph of me which might get into the papers. Also the description of the fight is for you alone, and not for the press. I am enclosing my captain's combat report and the message of thanks from the general commanding our army. So now I can close."

The report made by captain Kastner is as follows:

About 6 a.m. on August 1st Lieutenant Immelmann took off on a Fokker fighting monoplane in orde to drive away the numerous (about 10-12) enemy machines which were bombing Douai aerodrome. He succeeded in engaging three machines showing French markings in the area between Arras and Vitry. Heedless of the odds against him, he made an energetic and dashing attack on one of them at close quarters. Although this opponent strove to evade his onslaught by glides and turns and the other two enemy aircraft tried to assist that attacked airman by machine gun fire, Lieutenant Immelmann finally forced hi to land westward of and close to Brebières after scoring several hits on vital parts of the machine. The inmate, an Englishman (instead of an observer he had taken with him an number of bombs, which he had already dropped), was severely wounded by two cross shots in his left arm. Lieutenant Immelmann immediately landed in the neighbourhood of the Englishman, took him prisoner and arranged for his transport to the Field Hospital of the 1st Bavarian Reserve Corps. The machine was taken over by the section and will be sent off. THere was no machine gun on board. A sighting device for bomb-dropping has been removed and will be tested. A report on it will follow.

Signed: KASTNER
Captain and Section-leader.

The message of thanks from the general in command of the army:

On the morning of August 1st Lieutenant Immelmann of Flying Section 62 attacked a superior number of enemy aircraft, put several of them to flight, forced an English biplane to land and took its inmate prisoner.

I herewith express to Lieutenant Immelmann my high appreciation of this gallant deed and confer upon him in the name of His Majesty Our Emperor and King, the First Class of the Iron Cross.

Signed: von Pritzelwitz

IMMELMANN THE FIRST SCOUT

Although many German air victories had been already won in this first year of the war, this one obtained by my brother occupies a remarkable position in the history of the war in the air.

Firstly, it is unique in that it was gained by a pilot with so little experience and on his first flight in a one-seater fighter which he was flying for the third time. But, secondly, this victory is also a milestone in the history of German aviation, because it may be classed as the first victory by a pilot fulfilling the functions of a fighting scout.

The original purpose for which the Fokker pilots were to be used was that of supporting the C. and G. machines in the performance of their defensive work. The G. machines were equipped with two engines and two pivotable machine guns. At that time these aircraft belonging to the fighting squadrons had the task of keeping the front-line closed against the incursions of enemy bombing and reconnaissance aircraft and thus defending the German airspace. The two-seater C. machines, which differed from the B. machines by their more powerful engines and the machine gun served by the observer, were detailed to protect the unarmed B.s which were the actual working machines (artillery spotting, long-distance and close reconnaissances).

THE BIPLANE FIGHTER
AND THE FOKKER ONE-SEATER FIGHTER

When the 'Franz' (observer) and 'Emil' (pilot) made a good air-marriage, i.e. when their teamwork was good, these C. airmen sought encounters during or after their escort and reconnaissance duties, and in this fashion many opponents were vanquished. As we see from my brother's letters, such victories were won by his section and No. 20, which was also stationed at Douai. But all these victories gained by the C. crews may be differentiated from the later triumphs of the Fokker pilots by the fact that the crew of a C. machine divided the labour. The observer observed, and he alone handled the machine gun, so that in the case of a victory, he was the one who shot the enemy down. At that time the pilot of a C. machine was still without a gun; therefore he could only support his observer in a fight by means of a skilful approach to the enemy.

If the pilot followed the enemy's movements fairly skilfully when the two machines were flying at the same or different levels, even the most unexpected turns by the opponent left the observer with chances to attack him with his machine gun, which could be pivoted in all directions and keep him in his burst. The observer had no great difficulty in removing any gun stoppages while his pilot was flying the machine in such a way that enabled him to either break off the combat or maintain sufficient touch with the enemy to resume fighting as soon as the stoppage was cleared.

The methods of the one-seater were very different, because the pilot had to carry out the fighting activities unaided in addition to flying his machine and observing the ground and the movements of the enemy. But the fights waged by the first Fokker pilots required an extraordinarily cold-blooded and thrustful temperament. The rigid machine gun gave them only one direction in which to fire, so that it was not possible to aim at an opponent unless he was directly in front of the machine and more or less at a similar level. The fighting pilot had to aim with his whole machine, i.e. the incessant upward and downward movements of machines battling in air currents and the wide cone of spread of his machine gun made it absolutely necessary for him to hold his fire until he was within the shortest possible distance of his opponent.

If the gun jammed, it was imperative for him to break away from his opponent, because the removal of the stoppage generally required both his hands, and so he had to leave the machine to fly by itself. As our first fighting scouts usually went out hunting alone and found themselves opposed to enemy aircraft flying in formations, an attack on an enemy group demanded a lightning visualisation of the favourable possibilities and an ability to form a quick decision, if the pilot was to hold his own with his limited field of fire against the concentrated fire of the enemy's pivotable machine guns.

To this we must add the fact that the first fighting pilots were few in numbers and therefore received very large sectors of the front as their spheres of action. On the other hand the Aerial Defence Intelligence Service was not yet properly organised, so that these early scouts were often compelled to go hunting for long periods before they found opponents and then, perhaps, suddenly break off a fight because the small Fokker machine carried sufficient petrol for two hours only. This is the sole explanation of the fact that no other

Fokker pilot achieved a victory until after my brother's first one, although six old experienced pilots had flown Fokkers at the front for six weeks prior to it. It was, however, definitely impossible to employ these fighting pilots for offensive purposes, because the German inferiority in the air required that this elite corps should be used for defensive work, i.e., the Fokkers had to take their turns at barrage patrols with the G. and C. machines. But my brother's first war-flight on his Fokker was carried out as a hunting expedition. From the combat report sent in by his captain we may see that the purpose for which he took off was the pursuit and annihilation of his opponents, i.e., he hunted the enemy machines. Therefore we may class his initial victory as the first one achieved by a pilot fulfilling the functions of a fighting scout.

And so the first stone of the future scout flying was laid. The indefatigable zeal with which my brother searched the void for opponents in his Fokker and his indomitable will to attack made him an example to the little band of Fokker pilots, and in innumerable air encounters the German fighting pilots succeeded in gaining an aerial superiority.

IMMELMANN AND BOELCKE

Fired by the hunting zeal of his younger comrade of the air, Oswald Boelcke strove to emulate our Immelmann, and three weeks later he succeeded in gaining his first victory on a Fokker. Then began the competition between the two airmen, which amazed the whole world—friend and foe alike. In the Verdun area Boelcke played havoc with the enemy aircraft, while my brother lay in lonely ambush and stalked the airspace above Douai which the enemy avoided, so that it was seldom he could sight his prey and still more seldom that he could bring it to bay.

Unchanged as he was by all outward success, my brother steadfastly pursued his one and only objective—the destruction of his country's enemies and their banishment from the area which he had been given to guard. After thirteen months of strenuous fighting and patrolling activities he was as calm and purposeful when he took off for his last hunting flight on June 8th, 1916, as he was when he went up for the first one on August 1st, 1915.

THE FOKKER BECOMES KNOWN

"Douai, August 11th, 1915.
First of all, thanks for your letter. We are expecting to leave any day, because there is not much doing here now. According to the observations made by our infantry between Arras and Lens, there are no enemy machines in the air ten minutes after Boelcke and I have appeared. Those fellows are in a devilish bad way, and that's as it should be. Only one solitary airman has visited Douai since August 1st. When we arrived here in May, it was quite an understood thing for six to come along every day. That's how times have changed.

The weather also leaves much to be desired now. We can seldom fly at any time except in the evening, and the mornings are always foggy. Sometimes I fly the Fokker and sometimes the L.V.G.; I generally use the biplane in the morning and the Fokker in the evening. But it sometimes happens that I fly the biplane for three hours, land, get into the Fokker and fly it for an hour. Then the Fokker in the evening again, with airfights as the order of the day.

Several days ago Herr von Keller and I flew as far as Hesdin, a town which lies a fairly long distance behind the French lines. I get far more flying than anyone else in the section. I have managed to achieve quite a lot of records: (1) First of the section to cross the lines, (2) first to fly to St. Pol (a town west of Douai behind the French lines), (3) first to climb to 4,000 metres on an L.V.G. (4) record for the longest stretch flown in a westward direction, (5) the greatest number of flights, (6) the quickest climb to 3,000 metres on a Fokker.

Several days ago I turned turtle in my Fokker. The wheels were in the air, and I was under the machine. Everyone who saw the business thought I was dead. But that was not the case. I didn't hurt a hair of my head. The only damage was a smashed propeller. I was lucky.

You say you want to know the difference between an L.V.G. biplane and a Fokker monoplane. The chief difference is that the L.V.G. has a so-called static engine, whereas the Fokker has a rotary engine, i.e., in the L.V.G. engine the cylinders are placed beside one another (or, more properly, behind one another), whereas in the Fokker engine they diverge from one another in a star-shaped pattern, and the whole engine revolves. The L.V.G. weighs about 22 cwt. altogether, and the Fokker only 6 cwt.

The notes we drop are enclosed in little bags, which are weighted with sand.

Just one more thing to tell, and then I must close:

The chief of the general staff of the 6th Army Corps made arrangements with another flying section so that he could keep me with the 6th Corps even if No. 62 left Douai. Kastner heard about it and said he would chuck flying if I was taken away from him."

THE SECOND VICTORY

"Douai, September 11th, 1915.
All sorts of things have been happening again. First of all, I have received your letter, for which many thanks.

You want to know my present daily occupation? I can give you the following picture of the evening work: I take off on the Fokker about 6 or 6.15 p.m. and reach the lines at about 6.30 or 6.40, having climbed to something like 2,200 metres.

I am the only German fighting airman there (occasionally I meet Boelcke), but at that height I find about four Frenchmen and two or three Germans. Three or four Frenchmen are flying high above me. The Germans identify themselves by signal lights when I am still far off, so that I can save myself the trouble of flying close up to them to recognise the markings. Now I make for one of the Frenchmen. I manage to climb about 100 metres above him. The machines flying lowest (2,200–2,500 metres) are generally unarmed. They are directing their artillery. I fire about 40–60 shots, and then the first of them goes down in a hurried glide.

Then I turn to the others, but they go down before I can fire a shot. Meanwhile I have flown across the lines. The enemy artillery shoots at me like mad. The high flying foemen come at me from three directions; these are armed. I am defenceless as long as I am below them. Therefore I recross the lines as quickly as possible. The enemy machines never come across, but always turn back at the lines. Finally the artillery also stops shooting. I climb until I have reached the height of the highest foeman, and then I go for him. When I have fired 200 rounds, he decamps hastily. A fight of that sort generally begins at 3,200–3,400 metres and finishes at 2,000. But often the enemy goes down in such a steep dive that I do not need to follow him, for I see that he has got a dose. Then I turn to the second. By the time I have finished with him the third has usually bolted.

This daily picture seldom changes.

Only yesterday and the day before yesterday it was different. I forced an artillery flier down. At first there were three enemy fighters in the neighbourhood, but after a while only one. The machine was a huge thing, with two engines and two machine guns; it was 3,400 metres up and I was 3,200. I therefore screwed myself up a bit higher on our side of the lines, and crossed when I reached 3,400.

Suddenly I caught sight of Boelcke, who wanted to attack, but was much lower. He followed me. After I had fired 100 rounds, the enemy began to go down. Then Boelcke was able to attack him as well. The enemy was now between two fires; he went down in a series of very risky turns. He could not escape us.

After I had fired 250–300 rounds he made a hasty landing. Unfortunately he succeeded in reaching his own ground. Meanwhile we had come down to 1,900 metres, and it was pitch dark. So home! When we landed, we found they knew all about our success. Someone had telephoned that two Fokkers had shot down an enemy fighter.

The following day I forced two enemy aircraft to land. Boelcke joined in the fight with the second one.

We signalled to each other to fly home, because it was already dusky. Suddenly I saw an enemy biplane attack Boelcke from behind. Boelcke did not seem to have seen him.

As if by agreement, we both turned round. First he came into Boelcke's sights, then into mine, and finally we both went for him and closed up on him to within 50–80 metres. Boelcke's gun appeared to have jammed, but I fired 300 rounds. Then I could hardly believe my eyes when I saw the enemy airman throw up both his arms. His crash helmet fell out and went down in wide circles, and a second later the machine plunged headlong into the depths from 2,200 metres. A pillar of dust showed where he hit the ground.

So then home. It was almost dark. Flares were burning when we reached our aerodrome, we could see nothing of the aerodrome itself. Suddenly my engine stopped—run out of petrol. So a forced landing. I made a smooth landing in the darkness, climbed out and looked round for Boelcke. He had been flying behind me. Nothing to be seen of him. Finally—he had the same bad luck. Ran out of petrol and made a forced landing. We were welcomed with congratulations on all sides, for everyone had watched the fight and the crash which ended it through their field-glasses.

What is the reward of all these experiences Yesterday I was decorated with the Albrecht Knight's Cross. I am enclosing it—quite a charming order!

All sections here have a Fokker. We are the only one with two. The jealousy is naturally great, especially as some have none now, because the pilot in question has crashed it. We haven't bent a single wire of ours yet. Then several sections asked why we had two, and the staff officer of the 6th Army replied: 'Fokkers are nowhere in such good hands as in Section 62!'

FRONT AND HOME

And now for your letter—Franz has also written me a long one. From what he tells me the airmen of Flying Section 68 seem to be funny sorts of gentlemen. But only a few sections are as successful as No. 62. They have written me from the Dresden Technical High School to say I am the first of the school to get the I.C.1.

If 'no one' has any more confidence in the War Loan, then it is my particular wish that you should subscribe as much of my money as possible. The best thing you could do would be to subscribe the 1,500 marks. Furthermore, I shall send you about 300 marks each month, and that will make 1,200 by January. If you add another 300, you can subscribe 3,000 altogether. The last instalment does not need to be paid until January. Moreover I advise you to hold up your hands in horror whenever you meet anyone who has no confidence in the loan. Luckily we don't meet that sort of idiot out at the front. Foreign banks have participated, and yet there are Germans who have no confidence!

I would denounce for endangering public safety anyone I found saying such things. What use would the money I have saved be to me if the country went bankrupt because some niggardly louts have no more 'confidence' to put up the cash? They want a kick in the pants.

My little dog sends greetings once more and takes the liberty of enclosing his photo. He simply couldn't keep still for excitement at the idea of giving you pleasure."

THE THIRD VICTORY

An English aeroplane was shot down by one of our fighting pilots near Willerval (to the east of Neuville). The pilot is dead; the wounded observer was taken prisoner.—*Excerpt from the*

official communiqué issued on Sept. 22nd,
1915, by the Higher Command.

"*Douai, September 22nd, 1915.*
On September 21st, my birthday, I took off at 9 a.m. in my Fokker monoplane. I had no special orders, but wanted to protect a machine of our section which was putting our artillery on to newly located objectives by telegraphic signals. These artillery fliers are often disturbed by enemy fighters and must then retreat, because their only weapons are automatic carbines.

So I make arrangements with the crew of the other machine about the spot where we shall cruise. At 9.45 a.m. I fly my circles over Neuville village, as agreed. I am 3,100 metres up, and cannot see the other machine, which has arranged to climb to 2,500. That does not matter; it will certainly be there. The only trouble is that I cannot see it; probably it is masked by my wings. I go round and round, for a whole hour. The business begins to be a bit boring. For a long time I have been looking out on my right; when I peer out to the left again, I see—quite close behind me on my left—a Bristol biplane which is heading straight for me. We are still 400 metres apart.

Now I fly towards him; I am about 10-12 metres above him. And so I streak past him, for each of us has a speed of 120 kilometres an hour.

After passing him I go into a turn. When I am round again, I find he has not yet completed his turning movement. He is shooting fiercely from his rear. I attack him in the flank, but he escapes from my sights for a while by a skilful turn.

Several seconds later I have him on my sights once more.

I open fire at 100 metres, and approach carefully. But when I am only 50 metres away, I have difficulties with my gun. I must cease fire for a time.

Meanwhile I hear the rattle of the enemy's machine gun and see plainly that he has to change a drum after every 50 rounds. By this time I am up to within 30 or 40 metres of him and have the enemy machine well within my sights. Aiming carefully, I give him about another 200 rounds from close quarters, and then my gun is silent again. One glance shows me I have no more ammunition left. I turn away in annoyance, for now I am defenceless. The other machine flies off westward, i.e., homeward.

I am just putting my machine into an eastward direction, so that I can go home too, when the idea occurs to me to fly a round of the battlefield first, for otherwise my opponent might think he had hit me. There are three bullets in my machine. I look round for my 'comrade of the fray', but he is no longer to be seen. I am still 2,500 metres up, so that we have dropped 600 in the course of our crazy turns.

At last I discover the enemy. He is about 1,000 metres below me. He is falling earthward like a dead leaf. He gives the impression of a crow with a lame wing. Sometimes he flies a bit and then he falls a bit. So he has got a dose after all.

Now I also drop down and continue to watch my opponent. It seems as if he wants to land. And now I see plainly that he is falling. A thick cloud rises from the spot where he crashes, and then bright flames break out of the machine. Soldiers hasten to the scene.

Now I catch my first glimpse of the biplane I intended to protect. It is going to land. So I likewise decide to land, and come down close to the burning machine. I find soldiers attending to one of the inmates.

He tells me that he is the observer. He is an Englishman. When I ask him where the pilot is, he points to the burning machine. I look, and he is right, for the pilot lies under the wreckage—burnt to a cinder. The observer is taken off to hospital.

I fly off again, to the accompaniment of rousing cheers from about 500 soldiers. When I reach home, the men of the section lift me out of the machine and carry me (on their shoulders) to my tent with loud hurrahs.

Later on I visited the prisoner in hospital. He told me I had hit the machine many times without doing much damage until at last I killed the pilot instantaneously with a shot through the neck, whereupon the machine fell. When it crashed, it took fire, and he was hurled out in a high parabola. That saved his life, and he only sprained his feet and back. He said he fired about 400 rounds and was astonished at not hitting anything. That is more or less a picture of an airfight. Compare it with the official communiqué issued by the Higher Command on September 22nd, 1915: 'An English aeroplane was shot down by one of our fighting pilots near Willerval (to the east of Neuville). The pilot is dead; the wounded observer was taken prisoner.'

I have so much work to do that every day my section-leader says I must not fly so much, or I shall knock myself up. But it does me good, and I feel very well.

Really I have a lot more things to tell you and many questions to answer. I shall start writing every day again. Meanwhile I shall send you off this bit, for otherwise you will worry yourself too much."

AN EXCURSION AND A ROUGH LANDING

"Douai, October 11th, 1915.
If my calculations do not deceive me, this letter should arrive
at the right time—on your birthday the day after to-morrow.

So my heartiest congratulations from afar for your birthday festival. I am sure you cherished the secret hope that I
would turn up suddenly. I, too, contemplated this possibility, but it was out of the question because just now there happens to be a lot doing here once more. Therefore my best
wishes must hasten towards you from the enemy's country
instead. May the new year of your life bring the fulfilment of
all your wishes, some of which date back a very long time.
And one of the chief ones is to see peace in the world again.
To the accompaniment of the distant thunder of the guns I
call out three cheers for the birthday child, but good wishes
alone serve no one. Unfortunately, I am debarred by the
events of war from bringing you a birthday present. Well, I
shall at least and at last give you a more detailed account of
myself again, in the sure expectation that it will provide you
with a birthday pleasure.

One day Captain Kastner asked me if I would fly him to
Ghent. I naturally agreed; he himself is a Taube pilot, you
must know, and has never flown a biplane.

We took off at 10 a.m. It was bad weather; there was a
fog on the ground and a closed cloud-ceiling at 400 metres.
It rained at intervals.

We soon climbed to 400. We were just sailing over a fairly large wood when the engine gave out after we had been
flying for ten minutes. Other times I have flown for three
hours without the engine stopping. I went into a turn to

dodge the wood, and my efforts succeeded in getting the engine going again. But only for a short time. It struck work again almost immediately, so there was a forced landing for me. But where? There was only the wood and nothing but the wood. In a corner of it I saw a small meadow, so that was the place.

While descending I calculate how far the machine will go along the ground (from its impetus). But however I calculate and consider the matter, I come to the same result: I need about 25-30 more metres than the length of the meadow. Then the machine will go on into the wood, which means that it will be smashed up for certain, and probably we two as well.

There is only one way out of the dilemma: I must put the machine down so heavily that the wheels break off, and then we can't go on. Certainly she may go over on to her nose or turn turtle on us. Can't be helped.

So I go down heavily. Crack! I can hear a wheel break. Then the machine jumps up again, puts the engine into the ground and the tail into the air, and, slowly but surely, we turn over. We unbuckle our belts and scramble out.

There lies the beautiful bird, with her wheels upward. One wing is cracked off, the right wheel is broken, the propeller smashed to pieces. We have stopped not ten metres away from the wood. My captain congratulates me on the good luck. It was the only thing I could do, otherwise we should have been sticking on the trees.

We continued our journey by car, and stayed two days in Ghent.

The repairs to my damaged machine took almost three weeks. About the same time Boelcke had bad luck with his 100 h.p. Fokker. Part of his engine broke away in the air, with the result that the cowling, the engine and the propeller went to pieces and he had to land. The machine was not serviceable again till three days ago. Further-more, our auxiliary fighter was put out of action by engine trouble and finally my Fokker was so badly shot about in a fight that it was unusable for a long time. So 50% of our proud machines were out of action, and only one fighter was serviceable. And all these things happened just at the time of the Anglo-French attacks. It was like witchcraft. All of us here believe the French knew through their spies that both Fokkers were smashed up, for they have never been so impudent as they are now. They flew quite low—16 machines at once. And I had to look on.

The fight which I mentioned above took place on September 23rd, and was a hard one. I attacked a big English fighter with two engines and two guns some where east of Arras. In the course of the fray the fellow shot up my undercarriage, the bracing wires on the undercarriage, the oil tank, petrol tank, engine cowling, engine and fuselage. I heard the bullets whizzing by and the whistle of the various parts as they flew off, but nothing hit me.

DAYS OF HEAVY FIGHTING

Now all is well again. All the eight machines are serviceable. But no Frenchman or Englishman makes his appearance.

No one who has not experienced the days of the attacks made by the French and English between Arras and Lens can have any conception of them. The drumming of the guns did not stop for a single moment. The magnitude of the onslaught is best shown by the orders of the day found on enemy prisoners.

Those were anxious days, but our thin line held its ground. The attack was no surprise, thanks to our aerial reconnaissances. We reported as much as three weeks beforehand that the enemy was concentrating troops behind his lines. The places behind the lines which we photographed showed strong masses of soldiers, horses and columns. Enormous dumps of ammunition stood ready for use.

So we expected the attack. The enemy's losses verge on the fabulous. The English attacked in six or seven waves, but the success was practically nil.

Once more my heartiest congratulations. I shall drink your health in a cup of chocolate!"

THE FOURTH VICTORY

Lieutenant Immelman forced an English biplane fighter down from 4,000 metres to the north-west of Lille; this officer has thus brought down four enemy aircraft within a short space of time.
Excerpt from the official military communiqué of October 12th, 1915.

"*Douai, October 17th, 1915.*
Today I will give you a report of my last success. I am very pleased to have been mentioned in the official communiqué just on your birthday.

But let me tell my tale.

I went up at 2.45 p.m. to take over the so-called air barrage. I flew to Lens and Loos, and there met six English biplanes cruising between 2,200 and 2,500 metres; I fought them for half an hour without getting one properly in my sights. As soon as I was properly on to one, I was immediately attacked simultaneously by two or three others, so that I had to disengage by a bold nose-dive. After about half an hour all six flew home, without having achieved their objective of a flight to Lille. I flew about between La Bassée and Lens in order to screw myself up higher.

I was up to about 3,000 when I saw shell-bursts over Lille, i.e., there was an enemy machine over there. I flew off there at once, climbing to 4,000 on the way. Then I saw an English biplane over Lille, about 800 metres below me. I went down on to him in a steep dive. He saw me when I was about 500 metres away from him. He went into a turn at once and flew towards La Bassée. I was within 250-300 metres of him before he completed his turn; I fired and pursued him, firing continuous series of 20-30 rounds.

When I had sent out about 300 rounds, the enemy observer ceased fire. After about 400 rounds the machine fell, turning over the left wing several times as it plunged into the depths. I went after it at once in a nose-dive, so that I was always close upon its tail. The machine caught itself at 1,400 metres, i.e., after a fall of 1,500-1,700 metres, and went down in wide spirals to land. It ran into a row of trees when it landed. The pilot died soon afterwards; he had six bullets in him, while the observer (Lieutenant Leeson) had a slight leg-wound. The machine was completely destroyed.

I put the English machine gun out of action at the very beginning of the fight by a lucky shot.

Prince Ernst Heinrich of Saxony arrived while I was still inspecting the machine. He made me explain everything and finally invited me to dinner.

The only souvenir I have of this machine is a sparking plug.

Besides this, I am sending you the following bits of loot: two English pistols, one of which is burnt, an engine cylinder and an engine piston, both of which are shot to pieces. The pistol is from my first Englishman, the burnt revolver from my second and the cylinder and piston from my own machine which was shot up in the airfight of September 23rd.

Boelcke was transferred from our section to Metz at the end of September. Lieutenant von Teubern also, as his observer. It is a great pity. No one knows why."

THE FIFTH VICTORY

In an airfight Lieutenant Immelmann shot down his fifth enemy aircraft, a French biplane manned by two English officers, who were taken prisoners.
Excerpt from the official military communiqué of October 27th, 1915.

"*Douai, October 28th, 1915.*
My heartiest thanks for everything. The leather waistcoat is splendid. It made its first flight on October 26th, with the success of which you have read in the papers.

I shall now begin with the descriptions of my last airfights. I have already described Nos. 1, 3 and 4 (near Verlinghem, north-west of Lille, so that Nos. 2 and 5 are left over. I have had about 30 airfights in all. I remember now that I have described No. 2; it was the one with the man Boelcke attacked; his machine fell somewhere near Souchez when he was shot through the head, and his crash-helmet came away in the fall.

Then there was no flying weather for a long time. I had a fight again on October 21st, with a French monoplane. I forced him down, and then he crashed, but unfortunately on his own territory.

I took off at 9.30 a.m. on October 26th. I had just climbed to 3,500 when I saw an enemy airman fly over the lines by Arras and make for Cambrai. I let him fly on eastward for a while. Then I took up the pursuit, hiding behind his tail all the time. I followed him for about a quarter of an hour in this fashion. My fingers were itching to shoot, but I controlled myself and withheld my fire until I was within 60 metres of him. I could plainly see the observer in the front seat peering out downward.

Knack-knack-knack … went my gun. Fifty rounds, and then a long flame shot out of his engine. Another fifty rounds at the pilot. Now his fate was sealed. He went down in wide spirals to land.

Almost every bullet of my first series went home. Elevator, rudder, wings, engine, tank and control wires were shot up. The pilot (Captain C. Dalgy) had a bullet in the right upper arm. I also shot his right thumb away. The machine had received 40 hits. The observer (Lieutenant R. J. Slade) was unwounded. His machine gun was in perfect working order, but he had not fired a single shot. So complete was the surprise I sprung on him.

I could not resume my flight when the prisoners had been taken away, because my petrol was finished. When at last some petrol arrived at 6 p.m., it was so dark that I could not take off again, but returned home by car, towing the machine behind me, with its wings folded up.

I get on splendidly with my captain. When I shot down my fifth on October 26th, he literally wanted to embrace me.

No one knows why Boelcke went off at the end of September. He claims to have shot down five enemy machines, but one of them landed on its own territory. If I counted all those, I should have at least seven. I only count those which crash or land on our ground, and not those which land behind the enemy's lines.

If you were expecting a birthday present, I must ask whether you received the money I sent off on October 2nd. I sent 350 marks (for War Loan). As I get 460 marks a month altogether, I was left with only 110 marks, with which sum I can just manage for the month, but unfortunately it leaves me nothing over for presents.

Meanwhile, I have got another decoration. It is the Military Order of St. Heinrich. I got it on September 21st. On the 22nd I was invited to dine with Prince Ernst Heinrich of Saxony at Lille.

You must not expect that there will be a decoration for every machine shot down.

Now I shall no longer object to being written up in the papers, since I have seen how everyone at home follows my successes. It is amazing. I have received at least eighty congratulations.

It's incredible how much I am honoured. I simply cannot describe it. My mail has swollen vastly since I have become a famous man. Fame also brings its burdens. I can't get it into my head that I have done anything particular. Above all, do not part with my letters or photographs. You will fall into my eternal disgrace if anything of mine is published. The public citation which His Majesty has approved and granted will suffice for me. It is very late now. So good night."

MODESTY

The closing sentences of this letter of October 28th are characteristic of my brother's modest nature. His deeds and successes were sufficient in themselves, but he could not get it
into his head that he had done anything particular! Then we
see that neither his descriptions of the fights, which he wrote
for his mother alone, nor any photograph of him were to be
given to anyone lest 'they might get into the papers', as he
wrote on August 3rd.

Not until shortly before his death—when he was at the
height of his popularity and legends about him were in
process of formation—did he consent to the publication of
personal details, because, as he wrote, 'it will do no harm if
the errors which are becoming widespread about me, are
eliminated in this fashion'.

When we look back on those times, we—and especially
the laymen amongst us—are inclined to disregard the ines-
timable services of our anonymous reconnaissance fliers and
measure the worth of a 'war-pilot' by the list of his victories.
Then we note with amazement that my brother achieved
with his six or seven victories in 1915 a high measure of
popularity and fame to which Boelcke and Richthofen could
hardly attain in later days despite their considerably larger
totals of victories. At least they did not do so during the war.

There are two reasons for this fact. Firstly, the scouting
pilots of the last year of the war who flew in formations and
engaged enemy formations which covered one another in
fights and flights had a gun-fire efficiency which was six
times as great as my brother's. The preliminary conditions
required for a victory were therefore many times more

favourable than they were for the solitary fighting pilot of 1915 who went out hunting in the first type of Fokker, with only one machine gun, and an unreliable one, too.

PIONEERS OF THE AIR ARM

The decrease in the difficulty of achieving an air victory is shown by the fact that the 'Pour le Mérite', which is the highest German war decoration, was conferred for a total of eight victories up to the beginning of September, 1916, whereas in 1918 it was not awarded until after the thirtieth victory. Nevertheless a number of pilots succeeded in winning the 'Blue Max' (as the pilots nick-named the 'Pour le Mérite') in the latter year, while up to the middle of June, 1916, only three airmen held this high distinction.

A proof of the very great difficulty airmen of the earlier years experienced in converting any one of their numerous flights into victories or of even holding their own against the numerical superiority of the enemy is shown by the fact that none of the first fifteen Fokker pilots saw the year 1917! They are all worthy to have their names recorded in the history of German aviation as pioneers of the German air arm, but only the names of their two most famous representatives have become well-known—Immelmann as the first scouting pilot and his comrade Boelcke who succeeded to his inheritance and enlarged it.

But although the victories which were so difficult of attainment in those days may have laid the foundation of the fame won by my brother and Boelcke, yet the former's outstanding popularity was due to a success which no individual scout and indeed no Jagdstaffel achieved after him: the absolute aerial supremacy over a sector of the front. For thirteen months my brother was able to 'keep order', as he modestly expressed it, in the air space between Lille and Peronne, and in effect exercise an unconditional aerial supremacy there.

AERIAL SUPREMACY

He was generally alone when he went his ways in the heights, and whenever he saw an enemy machine in his territory, he pounced upon the intruder like a hawk. But our valiant field-grey soldiers that dwelt in the dug-outs of the 6th Army knew what it meant when they heard the rattle of machine guns high in the air and remarked with satisfaction: "Our Immelmann is giving it to another Tommy!"

For thirteen months he was the faithful watchman of the 6th Army, and only for a few weeks after his death did his Fokker pilots, led by his best pupil, Lieutenant Mulzer, succeed in keeping intact the aerial barrier he had built up in front of this sector. Then it collapsed at the beginning of the Battle of the Somme, and once again the enemy squadrons encountered practically no opposition when they pranced about in Immelmann's hunting grounds.

But innumerable flights and fights were my brother's lot before he won respect from his opponents, before the foeman who saw his approach knew that retreat was the best course under the circumstances, before enemy airmen avoided his domains as far as possible and before he had to poach on neighbouring sectors in order to win victories.

From October, 1915, onward the Englishmen on the further side of the barbed wire told one another that in the air over Lille there was an eagle into whose realm no other bird could venture unplucked.

The respect and admiration felt by the English pilots, who were always so generous in their recognition, led them to give my brother a nickname—an act of homage which only occurred once in the war—and this nickname characterised and acknowledged his faithful and successful activities so fully that it spread along the front and into the homeland with the speed of the wind. They gave him the name of the lord of the air: The Eagle of Lille.

III

The Eagle of Lille

THE SIXTH VICTORY

Yesterday Lieutenant Immelmann shot down his sixth enemy aircraft, an English Bristol biplane equipped with three machine guns, westward of Lille.
Excerpt from the official military communiqué of November 8th, 1915.

"*Douai, November 17th, 1915.*
I have just returned from a fight which was not only an unsuccessful one, but indeed proved very disadvantageous for me. In addition to a few trifling holes in my wings, I received two bullets in my engine which forced me to land.

I took off to hunt the English. For a long time I didn't see any. After a while I caught sight of an English machine which was being shelled from Douai. I was just over Arras at the time. When I met the enemy half way between Arras and Douai, I found three English machines, a large one and two of ordinary size. Being about 700 metres higher, I swooped on the rearmost and began the fight. He returned my fire at once. The rattle of our machine guns drew the attention of the other two, who turned round and also fired.

So I fought these three for a long time until at last I heard a bullet hit my engine. As chance would have it, my gun jammed at the same moment. My engine fell away so badly that I had to go down. I hope one of the three got something.

I am badly behindhand with my reports. I shot No. 6 down on November 7th. I haven't got any photos of this affair yet, but they will come along.

On November 7th I was once again doing my usual aerial patrol. Flying in the profoundest peace, I did several circles round Arras, and then I saw an enemy airman crossing the lines near Lens. He was about 1,000 metres below me; consequently I was able to push the machine down as I flew towards him and so approached at great speed.

I came up to within 100 metres of him. The Englishman had not yet noticed me, so I held my fire. I waited until within 60 metres and then gave him 50 rounds, whereupon he went down in a left-hand turn. An Englishman flying about 20 metres higher shot at me, but with no success. I went down after the machine I had attacked. After he had dropped several hundreds of metres in a glide, he fell. Shortly afterwards I landed near him. The machine was completely wrecked, both inmates were dead. I pulled the two bodies out of the wreckage. One had six mortal wounds, the other two bullets in his head. All their bones were also broken.

The aviation staff officer, who had watched the fight, came also to the scene of the crash. I was congratulated on all sides. When everything of military value had been removed from the two bodies, they were taken away for burial. I took off and flew home. There I had further honours paid to me. Congratulations came in from all I sides.

On November 14th I was commanded to attend a court banquet given by Crown Prince Rupprecht of Bavaria. The King of Saxony and Prince Ernst Heinrich were there. Other people whom I knew were His Excellency von Laffert, Wilsdorf, O'Byrn (Wing Adjutant) and several other high dignitaries of the Saxon forces.

Several days previously I received a telegram from War Minister Falkenhayn, congratulating me and informing me that the Emperor had conferred on me the Knights' Cross of his House Order. That was naturally something out of the ordinary, because the Hohenzollern House Order is a rarity. Boelcke and I are the only airmen who have it. There is only one other Saxon officer besides me who has got it. The King of Saxony also told me that it is quite a special distinction for His Majesty to confer, and that I could be particularly proud of it.

Several of the high and highest gentlemen kept me quite a long time in personal conversations, and I was continually asked to tell them details of my air fights.

I spent that night in Lille.

HONOURED BY THE KING OF SAXONY

The King intended to inspect Flying Section 24 a Saxon section led by Captain Rosenmüller, on the following morning. I was ordered to go out there and give a demonstration of flying. I had gone from Douai to Lille by air, and my batman went by train with the necessary luggage and the little dog.

I arrived at No. 24's aerodrome at 10 a.m. Two photographers promptly rushed at me and begged for the honour of taking my photo. I was very gracious to them.

I was snapped about twenty or thirty times and then filmed. The films will appear in all German cinemas in about three weeks' time. So you must go to the pictures diligently so as not to miss this film. I was first filmed with the fourth English machine I shot down, then with Captain Rosenmüller and finally in conversation with the King of Saxony.

All the machines of Flying Section 24 were drawn up in parade order. First came the English machine, then my monoplane and finally the ten machines of No. 24. The King arrived at 10.30 a.m. He went straight up to me, inspected and expressed surprise at Englishman No. 4, and then took a photo of myself standing in front of this machine—just imagine, the King snapped me himself. Several generals and excellencies did the same, but it no longer made such a great impression on me.

The film camera then put in some violent work when the King approached my machine. I explained everything, as accurately as possible in order to give some idea of my machine to those who were complete laymen in such matters. His Majesty showed visible interest in it.

When the King passed on, I donned my leather kit and prepared to take off. His Excellency von Wilsdorf had previously asked me to do no stunts and confine myself to ordinary flying.

When His Majesty had seen all the machines, I took off. I managed to make my machine leave the ground just in front of His Majesty. Then I went into several turns and glides, fired about 80 rounds in the air, made a short nose-dive and a steep climb, flew close above the ground in front of the King, saluting as I passed him, and then landed.

When the machine came to a standstill, the King snapped me again. Then he came up to me and expressed his appreciation of what he had seen. Suddenly he grew plainly embarrassed and said: 'It's really fine what you did, hm, hm, hm, hm. I've brought you something as well. Hm, hm, hm. There's a monoplane on it, haha, a monoplane.' And with that he handed me a plate of Meissen porcelain, on which there was a charming picture of a fight between a German 'Taube' and an enemy biplane. It is really quite nicely done.

Several biplanes then flew, but they could show no novelties.

His Excellency von Wilsdorf then told me that the plate was a special mark of distinction, because the King went into the Royal Porcelain Factory at Dresden himself and chose it. It is really very nice of him. Such a present is certainly a far more personal thing than an order.

I was invited to lunch at No. 24's mess. After the meal I visited my English prisoner from No. 24, who was still in Lille. I flew back to Douai about 5 p.m. My batman went back by train. The railway journey lasts an hour and a quarter, while I fly it in 12-15 minutes.

So now all these days of fame are over, but the consequences of the fame continue. My mail has risen to something enormous. Everyone wants a detailed report from me. It is quite impossible for me to answer even a portion of the letters. But you mustn't think that writing letters to other people will stop me writing to you. I never write the others more than a card, with my photo on it. I would never have thought that fame was bound up with such inconveniences. I cannot tell you all the minor honours that come to me daily and hourly from other directions. Now I will answer your questions.

Yes, everyone is surprised that I never went to a school for monoplane pilots. I have to say it, otherwise they won't believe it. You can send me grub any time; it is always welcome. I consider it impossible for any parcel to fail to reach me, because I get letters every day addressed: Flying Lieutenant Immelmann, Western Front, and that is quite enough."

LEAVE

Only on one single occasion did our family have the pleasure of seeing my brother home on leave. As he refused to take any leave because it would have meant quitting the front and the section which had grown so dear to him, the inducement must have been a special one. And so it was!

On November 28th, 1915, an exhibition of flying was arranged at the Leipzig aerodrome at Mockau, in order to raise funds to provide Christmas presents for all the airmen; it was also intended to convey as great an impression as possible of the progress made by our air arm. The promoters asked the general commanding the army to give my brother leave and wrote to ask him to take part in it. He replied: "I will not say 'yes' and I will not say 'no'; I shall be glad to come if my duties permit it." The army authorities granted him leave in view of the good cause.

The brilliant success of the exhibition proved the great popularity and affection won by the youthful pilot. At a lunch given before it the Mayor of Leipzig toasted my brother as the most important representative of the young air arm and presented him with a splendid silver cup made by Schneider, the great jeweller of Leipzig.

It was bitterly cold on the wide field of the aerodrome, and yet a crowd of many thousands attended. Who would have stayed at home when there was a chance to see the young flying officer whose deeds were in everyone's mouth, whose successes were reported daily by the official communiqué and whose mother dwelt within the walls of Leipzig?

At that time I was also attached to a flying section and happened to be on leave, so that I was able to accompany my brother to the aerodrome. Director Fokker also made the journey from Schwerin to Leipzig to greet the most successful pilot of his machines.

As, owing to a wish expressed by the military authorities

at the last moment—which he naturally considered in the nature of a command—my brother was unfortunately debarred from showing his own flying skill, Director Fokker exhibited his machine himself in most masterly fashion.

My brother was soon recognised by the crowd. There was no holding them then. He was quickly surrounded by a dense throng of enthusiasts, from whose ever renewed applause he had the greatest difficulty in escaping.

Even after so many years this day remains unforgettable for those who experienced it!

In the few following days of leave it was likewise practically impossible for my brother to show himself in the Leipzig streets. He was quickly recognised and made the centre of enthusiastic ovations.

But he did not let all this detain him long at home. He was not fond of such festal days. So he returned to the front even before the expiry of this leave, which was to some extent forced upon him. Ill-health would have been the only reason for a holiday which he admitted, but since he enjoyed the most robust health up to the day of his death, those Leipzig days constituted his entire leave. He did not come home again in the seven months which elapsed before his death.

THE SEVENTH

> Yesterday Lieutenant Immelmann shot down his seventh enemy aircraft, an English monoplane, in an airfight over Valenciennes.
> *Excerpt from the official military communiqué of December 16th, 1915.*

A VISIT TO BRUNSWICK

"Douai, December 20th, 1915.
Now I have been back here a fortnight without managing to write to you. When I left Leipzig, I had no idea of the train's route. I only knew that it would take me to Cologne, and that was enough. I was therefore no little astonished when I suddenly read 'Wolfenbüttel' on a station. That meant Brunswick must be the next station. I promptly inquired the possibility of connections from the ticket-collector in case I wanted to break the journey, and learnt that I could travel straight through to Lille by catching a night train at 1 a.m.

I couldn't have hit it better. So I broke my journey in Brunswick, with the intention of resuming it that same night. Aunt Elsa and Alma were delighted, and Ilsa had the surprise of her life when I went to take her home from school at 1 p.m. Naturally I had to tell them all sorts of things. The old grandmother and several other old ladies also came to listen.

When I wanted to depart, Alma and Ilsa were so obstinate in their pleadings with me to stay, that with the best will in the world I could do nothing but consent unless I wanted to appear absolutely heartless. I had to promise Ilsa that same evening before she went to bed that I would call for her at the school the following day without an overcoat (because of my decorations).

In the morning I looked in to say good day to the Küsters. Then I resumed my journey in the evening, feeling very pleased with myself and quite certain that my visit gave genuine pleasure to the Boetzels.

At Douai they were very astonished to see me return a day earlier than necessary. Practically nothing had happened in the section. There had been only two days of flying. A neighbouring section had shot down a French machine, which was exactly the same type as my No. 5.

On the following Saturday I was once more invited to dinner with the Crown Prince of Bavaria. Before we sat down to table, he invested me with the Bavarian Military Merit Order, with Swords. It was quite a small affair; we were only seven men.

THE FOKKER TURNS TURTLE

There was plenty going on in the next few days. Someone was always coming along to have a look at the two 'aces', for Boelcke rejoined our section about a week ago. He didn't enjoy himself with the 'Carrier Pigeons'.* Boelcke has got a 160 h.p. Fokker, and I am to fetch mine in the next few days. This machine, which is also a small monoplane, has a 160 h.p. engine that enables it to climb to 3,000 metres in 15 minutes and fly at 160-170 kilometres an hour.

Generally speaking, flying activities have been quite decent here. On December 12th I was forced to abandon pursuit of an enemy biplane, because my engine (100 h.p.) began to give out. Some small necessary repairs were done on the following day, and I decided to try out the engine that same morning (December 13th).

A fairly strong wind was blowing. I had just taken off and climbed to 40-50 metres when the engine dropped considerably and finally went dead. I made a forced landing on a ploughed field. When I was almost touching the ground,

* 'Carrier Pigeons'. The nickname given to the first two German squadrons of big fighting machines in order to camouflage their real activities from enemy spies. Translator's Note.

the wheels went into a deep furrow, and the wind got underneath the steering surfaces (I had to land downwind) and lifted the tail up. Slowly but surely the machine turned over. I huddled into the bottom of the cockpit and turned the petrol off. Then I waited.

I heard several mighty crashes, and then the bird was on her back. Feeling no pains anywhere, I knew nothing had happened to me. I unbuckled myself with some difficulty and tried to crawl out. But that was completely impossible. With all my efforts I could not manage to lift the 7-8 cwts. of the bus. So I resigned myself to my fate and waited. At last, after a long, long time some soldiers arrived who had seen my machine turn over. They lifted up a wing, and so I managed to get clear.

But what did the beautiful bird look like? The propeller was broken, the engine shaft bent, the fuselage split down the middle and both steering surfaces broken. So it was almost a total write-off. Soon a car arrived from the section, which had been informed of my mishap, and I promptly took off in another 100 h.p. Fokker.

That day there were altogether six English machines over Douai, and we couldn't manage to get one of them. There was also some lively flying on the 14th.

THE SEVENTH

The next day it was fairly foggy. The clouds appeared to hang pretty low. But you can never trust an Englishman, and so I took off in spite of the uncertain weather. It was fairly dark when I started, but half an hour later it was quite bright. I was up to about 200 metres when I saw the flashes of bursting shells or shrapnel in the far distance. They came from the direction of Lille, and the flare of the bursting shells stood out quite clearly against the dark sky. So off I went to Lille. When I was 10 kilometres away from the town I saw the enemy high above me to northward and on my right. I was only 1,200 metres up then, and he was 2,800, so that I was not able to attack him at the moment.

I am making you a little sketch of my pursuit. If you have a map, you will be able to follow it more exactly. I am sketching the whole thing from memory, so I make no claim to accuracy.

When he saw me, he did not fly southward, as was probably his original intention, but bore away from me in an eastward direction. I went into a turn and flew along-side him, although still much lower. He tried to reach the salvation of the lines by a right hand turn. I promptly flew towards him, although still somewhat lower and so unable to attack. I had climbed to 2,600 by then, but he was at 2,800. The feint attack I made on him misled him into abandoning his westward course and flying further south-east. Again he tried to reach his lines, but with a similar lack of result.

Now we were both at the same height, but I nevertheless let my machine climb a bit more. He did the opposite, for he put his machine down and thus obtained such a great speed that he almost disappeared from my view. I could only see him as a faint grey smudge on the distant horizon. He certainly hoped I had lost him, because he went into a right hand turn and headed for Douai.

I was now 3,200 metres up, while he might have been 2,600-2,700. As his line of flight was now about perpendicular to my own, my greater height enabled me to approach him at very fast speed. When we were still 500-600 metres apart, he opened a furious fire on me. The distance was too great for him to have any chance to succeed. He fired at least 500 rounds while I was coming up from 500-150 metres of him.

Then I too began to shoot. First I gave him a series of 40 rounds. The enemy flew gaily on; why not? Now there was only 100 metres between us, then 80 and finally 50. I saw the enemy observer fiddling at his machine gun. Probably he had a jam.

I had to use the moment. Without allowing the pause of even a fraction of a second, I let off 150 rounds. Suddenly the enemy monoplane reared up; with its propeller pointing skyward and its steering surfaces earthward, it stood on its tail for several seconds. Then it turned over by the right wing and whirled down in a nose-dive.

My efforts to catch another glimpse of it during the fall were useless. I flew a circle round the scene of the fray and then went off home.

Then I received a jubilant welcome, for a telephone message had already come through: 'In an airfight over Valenciennes a Fokker monoplane shot an enemy monoplane down. The latter turned over several times and crashed near Raismes, north-east of Valenciennes. Further details are lacking. The German monoplane went off in the direction of Douai.'

The section knew who was the victor, because I was the only one who had been up.

I asked our section-leader for permission to proceed to Valenciennes at once, which he granted. When I arrived there, I learnt that the wreckage had been cleared away and the bodies (Lieutenants Hobbs and Johnston) already buried.

I ascertained the following details from eye-witnesses. After dropping vertically for some distance, the machine turned over several times. In one of these turns the observer fell out when the machine was about 100 metres from the ground. He fell on to a tree. The branches pierced his body, which then dropped to the ground. There were several bullet wounds in his head and neck, so that his death must have been instantaneous.

The machine and the pilot were found about 500 metres away from this tree. The pilot had a couple of bullet wounds in his head, in addition to one in his chest and another in a leg. The machine crashed on to the wall of a house and was smashed to bits.

No gun was found in the machine. But I induced the men to make a further search, because I had heard the enemy's shots. Finally they discovered the machine gun a long way to one side; it had fallen out.

Then it became clear to me why the Englishman ceased fire. One of my bullets went through his barrel, while another destroyed the loading mechanism. These facts I naturally could not know when I was still in the air. After receiving congratulations from all sides, I returned to Douai.

There you have in brief the events of the last few days. Did you hang out your flags when the news of No. 7 came?

You hope I may be home for Christmas, but it is quite impossible. Yesterday I sent you two large photos, taken by P. They will have to be our Christmas surprise.

I am sending you 100 marks. I am sure you want something and would gladly buy it if you had the money. I really would have liked to buy something for you with it, but if I did so, the business would go to the French. And any tradesman at home would surely be glad to take the 100 marks. I am enclosing 50 marks for Elfriede She must buy herself something sensible with it. I know it seems funny to be sending you money, but I find it foolish to buy French vases or that sort of rubbish as so many do, and send them home.

I shall hardly write again before Christmas, because there won't be much happening up to then. So I wish you today a real good Christmastide!"

THE EIGHTH

Lieutenants Boelcke and Immelmann each shot down an English machine, to the north-east of Turcoing and near Bapaume.

In recognition of their magnificent achievements His Majesty the Emperor has been pleased to confer the Pour le Mérite Order on these two dauntless officers.

Excerpt from the official military communiqué of January 13th, 1916.

"*Douai, January 29th, 1916.*
I believe there is no need to assure you that my correspondence obligations have risen to something immeasurable. I receive 30-40 letters and postcards every day. Terrible. All the same I am going on well.

I don't remember where I got up to in my last letter. I certainly wrote you that I had received a silver cup, inscribed 'To the Victor in Aerial Combat' and that your parcel arrived somewhat late. But that hardly matters at all. Everything was in good condition and everything except the Christmas tree decorations could be used.

A bombing squadron came along on January 5th. One enemy belonging to it was shot down. Boelcke shot one opponent down in the morning. When the squadron arrived, I jumped hastily into Boelcke's 160 h.p. machine. I did not know how much petrol there was in it, and it was all gone by the time I climbed to 2,500 metres.

About 8.30 a.m. on January 12th when dawn was just giving place to daylight, news came through that enemy machines had crossed the lines in various places. So Osterreicher and I climbed into our Fokkers in the hope of catching one or other of them. When I was up to 500 metres, I saw Boelcke also getting in his machine. Then I saw no more of him, and didn't know where he had flown to. In any case we didn't hang about Douai, because we knew no more would turn up there, Osterreicher and I flew to Arras, and then bore off southwards.

I was halfway between Arras and Bapaume when I saw shell-bursts in the direction of Cambrai and stretching away to northward, so that apparently someone was trying to fly from Cambrai to Douai. I promptly turned eastward.

Osterreicher also appeared to have seen the shell-bursts. We were both about 3,200 metres up, while, judging by the shell-bursts, the enemy seemed to be between 2,600 and 2,800. We could not see the enemy aircraft at all, and the shell-bursts only with difficulty, because we were flying right into the sun, which was still very low. I had some trouble to keep on the right course. Osterreicher went off southwards.

That was the only reason why I reached the enemy machine before him; it was flying a west to east course. Before I could recognise the type he went into a sudden turn and headed due west. I was 3,000 metres up and he was 2,800. He appeared to have seen me. Why otherwise this sharp turn?

Now I recognised him. A Vickers biplane, with both pilot and observer in front of the engine. I dived steeply on to him, as he was now coming straight towards me. The observer fired at me from in front.

I could see their leather helmets quite plainly. The observer was kneeling behind his machine gun. So now it was up to me to get my machine round quicker than the enemy.

I went completely round before the Englishman started to go into a right hand turn. I was now firing like mad, but without results, for he completed his turn. But I went round again at once, so that I had him in the same position. I gave him about another 100 rounds.

Then all of a sudden a reddish-yellow flame shot out from his engine, leaving a long trail of smoke behind him. I ceased fire, and the Englishman went down in steeply banked turns, with his machine all ablaze.

I saw the machine make a smooth landing and someone jump out. Men who had been working a threshing machine in the neighbourhood hurried up. I landed in a meadow about a kilometre away.

The machine was set alight by spurting petrol, because I hit the tank several times. It caught fire at 2,200 metres, and was still burning when I arrived.

The observer was killed, but the pilot escaped with a slight wound in the head. He told me his observer lost his head completely and only fired 5 rounds, after which he was incapable of offering further resistance. I introduced myself and told him he was my eighth victim.

'You are Immelmann?' he then inquired. "You are well known to us. Your victory today is another fine sporting success for you.'

I then handed the wounded man over to a doctor, while

a section stationed in the neighbourhood took charge of the machine and its contents. I climbed in my cockpit; as the weather had grown worse, I flew straight home. I proudly reported my new victory to my captain. He congratulated me cordially and said: 'You are a fine fellow, and Boelcke also got one, somewhere near Lille, you know.'

I was never so pleased at one of Boelcke's victories as I was that day. Unfortunately, he had landed at Lille and was not yet back, so that we were unable to congratulate one another.

In the afternoon our captain put a car at my disposal, so that I could fetch the machine gun, ammunition, etc. I also took along a photographer, who made several snaps. We were accompanied by a very dear comrade, who, I regret, to say, was killed several days later in an airfight.

On our way to Bapaume, whither the debris and armament of the machine had been taken, we ran over three fowls, which we took along with us, and they made us a nice meal the next day when cooked with rice.

We got home fairly late, about 9 p.m. In view of the double victory it was not surprising to find champagne on the table and everyone in high spirits. But they had all dined, and only we late-comers were hungry.

THE 'POUR LE MÉRITE'

As is the custom when the section celebrates a joyful event, our leader spoke a few words, but this time his speech was livelier and gayer than usual. I cannot remember everything he said, because I was too excited with my pleasure. I did not really listen until at the end of his short speech. He said something about a milestone in the history of aviation and a turning point and recognition in high places, but finally the big word came out: 'His Majesty the Emperor has been graciously pleased to confer the highest war order, the "Pour le Mérite", on the two victors in aerial warfare.'

I was dumb. I should have thought it a joke if my section-leader had not said it in front of all our officers. I couldn't eat or drink anything that day; I didn't know whether I was awake or dreaming.

The next day congratulation followed congratulation, by telephone and telegram.

Those were days I can never forget. We were invited to dinner with the King of Bavaria, and a couple of days later with the Crown Prince of Bavaria, who gave us the Orders. The King of Saxony, the Crown Princes of Prussia and Saxony, Prince Sigismund, the Chief of War Aviation, etc., sent me telegrams of congratulation. They sent them to Boelcke as well. My mail swelled to 50 letters a day, and my batman became my 'private secretary'. At last, after a fort-night, things grew a bit quieter.

Boelcke attacked another Englishman on the day after our double victory, but this opponent succeeded in reaching his own territory. A few days later Boelcke left the section.

I arranged for my 160 h.p. Fokker to be sent straight here. So my trip to Schwerin is off. Thank goodness! I was terribly afraid of the long railway journey. The machine arrived on January 16th, and that was the best solution, because I was not obliged to miss anything.

So those, in a few words, are the experiences of the last few days.

You will see from the enclosed programme what I trained our men to do for January 27th. It was modelled exactly on a cadet display and received lively applause all round. I cannot describe to you all the individual items; it would take me too long.

CHRISTMAS

I have not yet written you anything about our Christmas festivities. We gave the men their presents at 5 p.m.; I enclose a photograph. There was a great abundance of presents, and they were all good ones. Then we received our own presents at 8 p.m. in the mess. I got two books, some sweets, some eau de cologne, all sorts of eatables and finally a silver travelling watch, engraved with the names of all the officers in the section. After that Boelcke and I received the silver cups which the Chief of War Aviation has had made for all who have shot down an enemy machine.

After the presentations we had a very tasty banquet. The evening went off as jollily as any Christmas festivity could do in war-time.

The New Year's Eve celebrations, to which we invited the officers of the Bavarian Flying Section, were just as nice and jolly.

Naturally that is the end of my decorations. They are quite enough for a simple lieutenant!"

SUCCESS AND COMRADESHIP

As a consequence of his opinion that he had 'done nothing particular', my brother was surprised every time he received a new mark of distinction. Although he attached no great importance to the numerous honours paid to him, the letters he wrote to our mother reveal the childish delight every fresh distinction gave him, even when he was at the height of his fame, and most especially when it represented the expression of some kindly thought. This we may see, for example, in the great pleasure afforded him by the personal note manifested in the Meissen porcelain decorative plate presented to him by the King of Saxony, Friedrich August III.

The particular satisfaction he felt at the conferment of the 'Pour le Mérite' Order was not unjustified, because he was the first Saxon to receive it. While still a young lieutenant, he had received this Order which may only be conferred on the man who has won a battle, while no Saxon general or field marshal had ever obtained it.

How difficult this distinction was to win may be seen from the fact up to my brother's death in the middle of June, 1916. Boelcke and Buddecke were the only other flying officers to obtain it. Shortly after his death it was conferred on Lieutenant Mulzer as well, the latter being the pupil so often mentioned in his letters who followed his example so faithfully and developed under his leadership into one of the best scouting pilots of the initial period within the space of six months.

In his letter of January 29th my brother mentions quite casually that he arranged a display for the occasion of the Emperor's birthday celebrations on January 27th, which was 'modelled exactly on a cadet display'. Thus in spite of all the claims on him and in spite of all external honours and successes he remained the same simple comrade who was just as ready to find time to contribute to the general entertainment on festive occasions as he was when he gave his acrobatic performances in the cadet days. In this connection it is interesting to note that the Crown Prince of Saxony told him at their very first conversation how he remembered his amazing feats as acrobat and trick cyclist at the cadet displays. This tribute, paid more than five years after the events, constitutes a great appreciation of his performances of those times!

RUMOURS AND LEGENDS

"Douai, February 5th, 1916.
It is really hoggish weather today. Not the slightest chance of any flying. So I hope I have time for the letter I have been intending to write you for a long time.

I do not need the fur coat here, for it is never really cold. The boots and slippers have arrived, likewise the packet with the little chocolate things. To speak frankly, it was awful stuff. I felt ill after eating three of them, I gave nearly all the rest of them to my little dog, who was not ill. I never go to the theatre in Lille, and don't even go here, although we have a theatre, a cinema and a circus in Douai. I could not feel justified in taking leave as long as I feel so bright and well and healthy as I do now. If this makes Elfriede sad, it is very regrettable, but cannot be altered.

Rumours fly about here just as much as they do at home. Someone often asks how I am getting on and whether it is true that I have been wounded, taken prisoner or shot down, or again if I have crashed, vanished or been reported as missing. G.H.Q. rang up to ask whether I had really left here two days ago, and I replied 'No—I have been here for the last eight months.'

Boelcke is only about 24 or 25, but I do not know his exact age. I have now got my new Fokker, but have had no chance to try it out in action.

If the English had a Boelcke or an Immelmann, they would make far more fuss about him. In that case not merely the Entente papers, but all the neutral ones would sing the praises of the wonderful French or English airman. They never come to Douai now, except sometimes in formations of ten. The French have been on strike for a long time. It has been said in the House of Commons and in a French meeting that the supremacy of the air is no longer in the hands of the French or English.

Your worried post card has just arrived while I am writing this letter and feeling extraordinarily well. You can be quite sure of this—if anything really happens to me that might give you occasion to worry, the captain would inform you about it at once.

Frau K. has sent me a 'kitchen loaf'. A crazy affair! Not even my little lap-dog would eat it.

I believe all these many rumours will be the death of me."

THE NINTH

East of Douai Lieutenant Immelmann shot down his ninth aircraft, an English biplane containing two officers, one of whom is dead and the other severely wounded.
Excerpt from the official military communiqué of March 3rd, 1916.

"*Douai, March 16th, 1916.*
I am glad I haven't yet sent you an account of my 'ninth', because now I can make you a collective report.

No Englishman had been seen over Douai since February 5th. On February 19th my engine sustained damages which took three days to repair. It would almost seem as if the English knew it, for on the morning of the 20th four of their machines flew over Douai on their way to Valenciennes. I had to look on inactively.

At last some more arrived on March 2nd. I went up that day to take over the air barrage between Lens and Arras. I was about 2,200 metres up when I suddenly saw an English biplane heading for me. It was about 2,400 metres up, and close behind it, about 100 metres away, there was a monoplane. A Fokker, I thought, and rejoiced at the idea that it was going to shoot the Englishman down. But it did not shoot.

I took my glasses and saw (by the markings) that it was another Englishman. The next moment the two of them came down on me, firing as they dived. Being 200 metres below them, I was defenceless.

I escaped their onslaught by a nose-dive of 100 metres and flew a bit to westward while the Englishmen were flying east. Then I went into a swift turn, which brought me out behind my opponents. They were 2,200 metres up and I 2,100.

Then the pursuit began. The two of them were flying straight for Douai! The distance between us increased continually. My engine was running badly. I thought it most necessary to climb, but the Englishmen climbed as well. The two of them were up to about 3,000 metres over Douai, and I was 2,800. It was absolutely imperative for me to get up higher if I meant to attack them, or to at least reach their height. I considered whether it would not be better for me to land, for I could do simply nothing with my engine.

The two flew on towards Valenciennes. Finally they looked only as big as flies. I got all the climb I could out of my engine; as there was no hope of overhauling them, I meant to cut them off on the way back. I succeeded in that and met the couple half way between Valenciennes and Douai. I was now 3,200 metres up and they were 3,100.

Then the fun began. The English biplane led, followed by the monoplane which had a device for shooting through the propeller that seemed similar to my own. I put my machine behind the monoplane and began to shoot. He on his part tried to get on to my neck. He planned to put himself behind me by means of a wide turn, and I used the moment to attack the biplane. Keeping one eye on the monoplane, I shot at its companion everything I could get out of my gun. In this way I forced the biplane down to 2,500, whence it descended in a steep glide and landed. It was not advisable for me to turn on my other enemy, the monoplane, after that, for firstly I could not make up the lost 500 metres of height with my bad engine and secondly I had a gun jam. So I let the monoplane buzz off in the direction of Lille and went home.

News had already come through by telephone that an Englishman had landed at Souain. After receiving congratulations on all sides, I asked for a car. As chance would have it, Lieutenant Claus, an old friend of the cadet corps, had come along to pay me a visit while I was still in the air. We drove off to the landing place together.

The pilot (Lieutenant Palmer) had been bandaged and was sitting in a car. He had a wound in his foot. On a stretcher close at hand was the body of the dead observer (Lieutenant Burdwood). There were many bullet wounds in it. The machine had landed undamaged; it was dismantled and sent along to our section.

The machine carried two guns. The pilot used one of them to fire in front, just as I do, while the other was manned by the observer in the rear. The second machine gun was missing. It had fallen out of the dead observer's hands and was found several kilometres away from the landing place.

The Englishman said: 'Well, if I have been shot down, I am at least glad that Immelmann is my conqueror.'

We then drove back, to the accompaniment of cheers from the assembled crowd. Then we visited the Englishman in hospital in the afternoon. The machine was quite a new type, making its first flight at the front.

Several days later Crown Prince Boris of Bulgaria arrived. I was presented to him. Then several machines showed off a bit in the air for him. Finally he was photographed arm in arm with me.

On March 10th we all went home at noon, because of the bad weather, and no one thought there would be any flying. Just as we were at lunch five large English machines came over. There was no one on the aerodrome to chase them away. Another officer and I went off at once in a car, but when we got there, the birds had flown. Our biplanes ought to have made a revenge flight at once, but as the weather grew worse, it couldn't be done.

I felt very wretched all the day. I was very feverish all night; I believe I must have got a bit poisoned through inhaling burnt engine gas. I ate nothing all day, went to bed at 5 p.m., took a very hot bath, and perspired for an hour. I did not get up the next day, and only ate a bowl of gruel; on the day after I felt quite rejuvenated. I have been feeling very well ever since."

A DOUBLE EVENT:
THE TENTH AND ELEVENTH

Lieutenant Immelmann shot an English machine down eastward of Arras and another westward of Bapaume. The occupants were killed.
Excerpt from the official military communiqué of March 14th, 1916.

THE TENTH

"Ever since I have been a fighting pilot I have cherished the wish to settle two opponents on one day. This wish of mine was fulfilled on March 13th.

I took off at 12 (noon) in company with another Fokker pilot, Lieutenant Mulzer, to keep order in the air further south. Several minutes later I saw our batteries firing on an enemy airman to the south of Arras. So off I went there. When I arrived, I saw a German biplane and another one about 100 metres above it. As they were doing one another no harm, I thought the second one must be a German too. Nevertheless, I flew up and finally spotted the cockades. Now for it, I thought, and fired ... peng ... peng ... peng ... and then, after a few shots, my gun jammed.

I turned away from him, cleared the gun and made another attack. Mulzer had arrived by then, and he joined in. So now we concentrated our fire on him. I sent out 700 rounds of continuous fire, while Mulzer let off 100. Bump! down he went like a stone into the depths and came to earth at Serre village. Naturally both the inmates were killed and the machine completely wrecked. The remains lay so near the firing line that the English bombarded them with their artillery to prevent us going there. So we were unable to see the results of our work.

Shortly afterwards I had another fight with an English biplane. But unfortunately he got home.

We flew home, feeling pleased with ourselves. I landed first and promptly made my report. Mulzer did not see the machine go down and thought it crashed on English ground. We did not learn it was on German territory until we rang up to ask. Then I was naturally very happy. No. 10 at last! The double-figure series has started.

THE ELEVENTH

The 13th was a spring day—as beautiful as any described by the poets. The biplane airmen had gone off into the town; only the three Fokker pilots, Lieutenants Mulzer and Weber and myself were on the aerodrome. A war artist, O. Graff, had come there and was painting us as we lazily sunned ourselves in our comfortable canvas chairs. But we all had only one wish—for there to be 'something doing'.

And so it went on until 5 p.m. We were intending to go home soon. Suddenly the telephonist came running up: 'Five enemy aircraft heading for Douai from direction of Arras!'

'All machines ready at once!' were the orders. Unfortunately, the business took a quarter of an hour for me, because something had been broken earlier on in the day. There was nothing more to be seen of the five enemies. I rang up to inquire where they were, and received the reply that they had turned off in the direction of Cambrai. I called the news out to the other two and climbed in. They were up to 1,000 metres by the time I got off the ground at last.

Were we going to find them? In my opinion the other two were bearing too much to the left. I kept more to the right and pushed through the clouds at 1,200 metres.

For a time I saw nothing until I was out of the clouds. Then I looked ahead and saw four enemy aircraft flying westward at a height of about 2,000 metres. So one less already, I thought. I was determined to get the utmost climbing capacity out of my machine.

At last I was on their level or a trifle higher, perhaps. I drew closer and closer to them. We were almost over Arras.

Was I to let them escape me? Taking careful aim, I let fly 300 rounds at the one furthest on the right. Suddenly he went over on to his right wing. I gave him another 200; then he plunged into the depths and after turning over three times in his fall, crashed close to the village of Pelves, east of Arras.

I flew home at once. I received congratulations from all as I climbed out. They had watched the enemy go down from the aerodrome.

The two inmates were dead. The machine was a Bristol biplane. So I shot down my eleventh victim after a twenty minutes' flight.

The bodies had been removed by the time I arrived in a car. I did not see the machine, because it was already too dark, and so I never had a chance to photograph the remains. An anti-balloon gun wanted to dispute the victory with me, claiming to have shot it down, but its crew were finally made to see that this was not the case.

Then I heard in the evening that Boelcke had shot down a Frenchman on the 12th and another on the 13th. These two, however, did not fall on German territory, but on

French ground. There is said to have been great joy at G.H.Q. over this new double victory.

On March 14th I was out on patrol again at noon.

So those are my experiences.

I must also mention that the German Academical Automobile Club has presented me with a gold tie-pin, set with diamonds. Nice of them, isn't it?

I have now gained three victories in my new machine. I must tell you about another triumph which has pleased me monstrously. My old 80 h.p. Fokker (the machine with the factory number E 13), in which I finished off my first five Englishmen, is going to be exhibited in the Zeughaus Museum in Berlin. Isn't that splendid? So one honour follows upon another.

I have heard from other sources that I have been once murdered in Douai and once run over by a car! You may be convinced that you would be the first to hear of any accident that happened to me. Anyhow, let us hope for the best. You can laugh at all these evil rumours.

My captain has promised me himself that he would let you know of anything at once. I hope this promise will suffice to render you proof against all such stupid rumours. The reconnaissance flight to the Argonne with the biplane is naturally another piece of nonsense. I have never been out of Douai for a single day.

Nothing particular happened today. I did not go up. So once again I have given you a small picture of my activities."

THE TWELFTH

In an airfight east of Bapaume Lieutenant Immelmann disposed of his twelfth enemy aircraft, an English biplane. The crew were made prisoners.

Excerpt from the official military communiqué of March 30th, 1916.

THE THIRTEENTH

The English lost three biplanes in an airfight in the vicinity of Bapaume and Arras. Two of their crews were killed. On this occasion Lieutenant Immelmann shot down his thirteenth enemy aircraft.

Excerpt from the official military communiqué of March 31st, 1916.

QUESTIONS AND ANSWERS

"Douai, April 8th, 1916.
Let me give you a picture of my literary activities. Before me lie no fewer than nine communications from you. Furthermore, I must answer with letters 25 communications from God knows whom; there are another 25 for which postcard answers will do, and finally, there are yet another 35 which I have just answered.

After these introductory remarks I must plunge into the answers to your questions, and then I will tell my tale.

First I must say that I have received all the consignments of vegetables you mentioned. My best thanks also for the delicious candied fruits. I am still ill from them; they were absolutely splendid.

I can only shoot ahead with my machine gun, and straight ahead, in fact, because it is not pivotable.

Lieutenant Leffers is further southward. Bapaume, where I have been busy so often, belongs to his sector. Since there is nothing more to be found in our own area, one has to poach on the hunting grounds of others. Baron von Althaus is still further southward, and Parschau another bit further on (Verdun). Berthold is further away to the north. So far each of these has shot down four opponents. I know Parshcau and Leffers. Last June Parschau was the first to get a Fokker. Leffers has been flying a Fokker since the beginning of December. Our territories are marked off exactly by the trenches. Naturally the artillery shells us if we come within its range. Altogether I have now done about 450 flights so far.

Not long ago I got the Hanseatic Cross. Some time in the middle of March I had to undertake the aerial defence for the Mayor of Hamburg, who was visiting the Hamburg regiments. Wherefore, possibly because he was glad no enemy aircraft appeared, he gave me the cross. It is a very handsome decoration.

Boelcke has been a full lieutenant since February 18th, which was about the time when he shot down his 9th. He has been an officer since 1910, so that he got his commission about the same time as my contemporaries in the cadet corps. He is just as little a 'peculiar man' as I am; he is a very decent fellow.

So now I come at last to my report. My last one went up to my tenth and eleventh victories, i.e., up to about March 14th.

I have already mentioned that the ruling mayor of Hamburg was there on the 15th and invested me with the Hanseatic Cross. The weather was bad for a long time—not definitely bad, but dubious and unsettled, and that is the most unpleasant kind. You always have to be ready to go up, and yet you don't get any flying.

THE TWELFTH

At last we had glorious spring weather on the 29th. The sun seemed to be unusually warm for the time of year. We were just going to take off on a small barrage patrol when an orderly brought a wireless message that six enemy aircraft were coming to Douai from the direction of Arras. I was the first of the three monoplanes to go up. I climbed to about 1,000 metres, and then I saw two enemy biplanes. I couldn't yet recognise the type, because the distant visibility was very bad. The air was not clear, but milky-whitish. I went into a turn, in order to gain time to screw myself up. My opponents were flying at about 2,800 metres.

Now I see the others. Two are much further ahead, but only 2,500-2,600 metres high, and then, about 2 kilometres behind them, the two I first saw, and a fifth about 3 kilometres behind them, but about 3,000 metres high. I cannot see the sixth at all.

Well, there is sufficient choice for me among the five. I have great difficulty in keeping them all in sight, because the visibility is so bad. Before reaching Douai, they bear off right, as if to make for Courtrai. I likewise fly southward, climbing all the time, but keeping myself somewhat to westward of them.

I overhaul them a bit to the west of Cambrai. I am higher than Nos. 1 and 2, but still lower than Nos. 3, 4 and 5. My fear that they may escape misleads me into opening fire on No. 2. But I soon see the futility of starting the fray this way and leave him alone.

I must add that all five belonged to the Farman type. The structure of this machine permits the gunner an effective frontal fire in an upward or downward direction; he can also shoot to the right or left, but to rearward he can only shoot in an upward direction. I adapted my tactics accordingly.

I continued to climb, and after a while I had No. 3 in a favourable position in front of my gun. I was at a disadvantage in that I had Nos. 4 and 5 behind me. No. 5 was about 300 metres higher, and so could not do me much harm, and I was therefore left with No. 4. I made haste to put a packet of 100 rounds into No. 3's bus, with the result that he promptly went down in a steep glide. Feeling firmly convinced I had hit him, I did not worry about him any more, but turned to No. 4, in the hope of inducing him to descend as well. Unfortunately, I had shot away so much ammunition in my futile attack on No. 2 that I suddenly found myself without a single cartridge just at the moment when I hoped my onslaught would send No. 4 down.

So I had to let No. 4 go his way in peace. For the moment I was satisfied with one victim.

I flew home and ascertained by telephone that the enemy had landed at Bethincourt, not far from Bapaume. My captain and I went off at once in a car to see him. We found the machine standing somewhere south of the road between Cambrai and Bapaume, not far from Bethincourt. It was a biplane of the latest Farman type, but an awkward machine. The engine was a clumsy imitation of the Austro-Daimler. Altogether it made a very poor impression.

My bullets had slit up long strips of the wings and shot away two control wires. Likewise the carburettor and the cooling cap of one cylinder were hit, the radiator was holed several times and two valves and a tail wheel were shot to pieces. I had wounded the pilot in both arms, but the observer was an unwounded prisoner.

When they were taken prisoners, the pilot said he knew before he took off that he would be shot down that day. My fire made him nervous; as soon as I started, he switched off his engine in order to land. He made a grab at his Very pistol to signal me his intention to land, but at that very moment I put bullets through both his arms. The observer lost his head completely and did not fire a single shot from either of his machine guns.

We removed everything that was of value to us and then drove home.

I was mightily pleased with this success, for firstly I received a letter in the Emperor's handwriting, and secondly the King of Saxony said: 'Well, if Immelmann shoots down his twelfth, I'll give him something really fine. I've a surprise for him.' I was naturally very eager to know what it was.

The next day there was just as good flying weather. I took off about 11 a.m. to fly a brief hour of barrage. I turned off at once in the direction of Bapaume, for there is nothing more doing in our sector. When I arrived, three machines were cruising over the line to the south of Arras, two being about 2,600 metres up and the third 3,000. The two lower ones crossed the line and flew east. I hurled myself with a shout (figuratively) on the machine flying further away to northward. When I attacked, he promptly turned westward in order to reach the safety of the lines. That, naturally, he could not be allowed to do.

THE THIRTEENTH

I succeeded in putting an ample burst into his machine. Up to then the enemy observer had returned my fire pretty well, but now his machine gun remained silent. At first the machine dipped a trifle, then more and more, until it finally fell headlong. I did not go down after it, because there were still two others about, but I followed it with my eye, and so I saw the machine fly level again for a little while when close to the ground, and then go down hard and smash up. Unfortunately it had chosen such an unfavourable spot for landing that we could not reach it in the car.

An infantry regiment stationed there attended to the inmates and salved the remains of the machine. I had killed the pilot with a bullet through the heart, and the observer died from the effects of the crash.

After seeing the first machine fall, I promptly attacked the second. But he had already smelt a rat and vanished. I overhauled him just before he reached the lines and bombarded him vigorously. After a while he went down and reached the English lines in a steep glide. According to reports sent in by observation posts in the front lines, somewhere west of Serre.

Feeling satisfied with these results for March 30th, I flew home; I was happy to have scored another success. I then heard with joy that another gentleman of our section had also shot down an English machine—a Vicker's biplane. At last my number was up to Boelcke's again. My captain was naturally very pleased.

THE EMPEROR'S LETTER

Then in the afternoon came the very kindly telegram from the King of Saxony, followed on the next day by the letter from the Emperor. In this letter it is interesting to note that His Majesty has altered the word 'twelfth' into 'thirteenth', because the course of events has made twelve one too few.

The letter is as follows:

> 'I learn with pleasure that you have put out of action another enemy machine, which is your thirteenth. On this occasion I am happy to express once more my fullest appreciation of your excellent achievements in aerial warfare. Not long ago I showed you the importance I attach to your valiant deeds by conferring upon you my highest War Order, the Pour le Mérite Order.
>
> G.H.Q., March 30th, 1916.
>
> Signed: Wilhelm.'

Finally I received instructions to report to the Crown Prince of Saxony, who gave me the King's 'surprise', which turned out to be the Commanders' Cross of the Order of St. Heinrich. He was very affable and spoke of the cadet corps days at once. Then he asked me to lunch in the mess, where His Excellency von Laffert spoke some words of appreciation and called upon those present to give three cheers for the new Commander of the Order of St. Heinrich. After the inevitable photographs had been taken, I went off back to Douai, feeling pleased and happy. The Commanders' Cross is an eight-pointed star, in white enamel like the 'Pour le Mérite', with a picture of St. Heinrich in the middle and the royal crown above it. It is worn round the neck, like the 'Pour le Mérite'.

To me as a Saxon the Commanders' Cross is a higher Order than the 'Pour le Mérite'.

On my way through Lille I met Claus, and went with him to a café, where I wrote you the letter-card.

On my return to Douai I was met with sad news. A biplane belonging to our section was shot down by the English. The crew are dead. Moreover a monoplane of our section which was up on a test flight crashed close to the aerodrome and was completely burnt. We buried the poor fellow yesterday. The bodies of the other two fell into English hands.

Since the successes of March 29th and 30th mentioned above the English have no further desire to fly over here. We had perfect weather up to April 4th, but there was not a sign of an Englishman. Our losses, however, are somewhat too heavy.

I enclose with this letter a telegram and His Majesty's letter.

My batman and I have been in our seats all day, writing till our fingers were sore.

Finally I will give you my complete address.

The Royal Saxon Reserve-Lieutenant.
Herr Max Immelmann,
Pilot in Flying Section 62,
Commander of the Order of St. Heinrich,
Knight of the Ordre pour le Mérite,
Knight of the Iron Cross, First and Second Class,

Knight of the Military Order of St. Heinrich,
Knight of the Albrecht Order, with Swords,
Knight of the Hohenzollern House Order, with
     Swords,
Knight of the Bavarian Order of Military Merit, with
     Swords,
Holder of the Friedrich August Silver Medal,
Holder of the Hamburg Hanseatic Cross,
Field Post Station 406.

So now there is an end of the knighthoods and I close my
short letter with the hope that it will find you all in the best
of health."of health."

IMMELMANN AND THE '13'.

"Douai, April 24th, 1916.
It is Easter Monday and glorious weather. For which and
other reasons I am in the best of moods.To answer your
questions: I came to Douai on May 19th, 1915. Our section
was pronounced ready for active service on May 5th, 1915,
and left for the front on May 13th (Ascension Day), arriving
at Pont Faverger on May 16th and leaving again for Douai
on the 18th. I did not make my first flight on the 8th but on
the 21st of November. I was a pupil until March 26th, 1915,
the day on which I passed my final tests, so that I have only
been a pilot since the end of March, 1915. I was never at a
monoplane school, which surprises everyone.

What events have happened on 13ths? I was transferred
to aviation on Friday, November 13th (two crashed to their
deaths on that day), and Flying Section 62 went off to the
front on May 13th. I was first mentioned in the communiqué

on October 13th. I scored my first victories on the Fokker E.13. I shot down my first brace on March 13th. I received His Majesty's letter on the occasion of my 13th victory.

My No. 2 crashed near Souchez, at a time when our troops were close to the town. I do not employ any tricks when I attack. I have also been photographed with the Crown Prince of Saxony.

Unfortunately two Fokkers lost their way and landed on English territory. One Fokker has been shot down, and the French have reported the fact.

I really meant to answer your letter with only a short one, but once again it has grown much longer. But now I will tell you a few things.

THE FOURTEENTH

I must have got up to the middle of April in my last letter. Unfortunately there was very little flying weather.

On April 23rd I took off to fly a barrage with Lieutenant Mulzer, who is also a Fokker pilot of our section. After flying for an hour, we sighted an English biplane, which we attacked. Lieutenant Mulzer arrived a bit sooner and attacked him first. Then I came along too and fired about 120 rounds. We went on pursuing him until at last he landed at Monchy, near Arras. I was delighted at getting No. 14.

ON THE ACTIVE LIST AGAIN AND FULL LIEUTENANT

When I began to get known, the determination to remain an officer-pilot after the war matured within me gradually, and it was partly based on purely superficial reasons. The more known I became, the more I liked the idea. When I was with the Crown Prince of Saxony, we came to speak on that point. He showed visible pleasure when I said I was contemplating the idea of applying for reinstatement on the active list and told me my commission would certainly be well ante-dated. So I made my application and lo! it was granted only 18 days after I sent it in, and I was promoted from subaltern to lieutenant. The King is said to have been counting on my application and to have remarked: 'Of course we'll make him a full lieutenant at once!' So now I have re-entered the ranks of my former comrades.

Now I am a full lieutenant and all of a sudden one of the 'senior' comrades. It has been a quick business! I think my military career is unparalleled. Only a year ago I was an 'acting officer without a distinction' and today!! Do you remember how Franz always said it was incredible that I was not an officer and that I ought to do something to see that I got promoted? I always said: 'There's time for that yet!' When my first successes came, I was often asked where I would not like to be reinstated on the active list. I always replied: 'There's time enough for that yet!' And how glad I am that I have waited so long, for if I had sent in my application before I was so well known, my commission would not have been so much ante-dated. Now I have regained practically all my former seniority; there's a difference of a few days only.

Then we had a bit of a festivity in the mess that evening. To celebrate my promotion, they engaged a band, which played all through the meal. Hundreds of soldiers stood in the street and listened. Naturally they also ascertained the reason of the serenade. Then they all shouted enthusiastically: 'Immelmann, Hurrah! Hurrah! Hurrah!' After that we sang the airmen's march and 'Deutschland über alles'. When the strains of the latter died away, I called for three cheers for His Majesty, in which hundreds of male voices joined enthusiastically. Altogether it was a happy occasion."

SEVERE FIGHTING IN THE AIR

"Douai, April 25th, 1916.
I had a nasty fight in the air today. I took off at about 11 a.m. and met two English biplanes southward of Bapaume. I was about 700 metres higher and therefore came up with them very quickly and attacked one. He seemed to heel over after a few shots, but unfortunately I was mistaken. The two worked splendidly together in the course of the fight and put eleven shots into my machine. The petrol tank, the struts on the fuselage, the undercarriage and the propeller were hit. I could only save myself by a nose-dive of 1,000 metres. Then at last the two of them left me alone. It was not a nice business. But my machine will be serviceable again to-morrow.

On returning from this fight I received your letter and the jolly photos. I have also received two photos from Franz. The one of his crash is quite good, but it is a pity you cannot see quite all the left wing. My heartiest congratulations to Franz on passing his war pilot's tests. With that he has gone a good stretch of the way.

What is the replacement section in Altenburg, where he is? It is quite correct that the pilots' training has become considerably harder, because the standard required for active service flying is so much higher.

I myself took seventeen days over my first tests. (During the time I was Johannistal, I flew on seventeen days, so that only these can be counted.) I had one crash in Adlershof and two when I was with No. 10 in Vrizy, but one was quite a minor affair.

I have already told you about the airfights in which I got the worst of it—twice in the biplane and three times in the Fokker.

Although we have had the most glorious weather for four days, no Englishman has turned up in our sector."

ONE YEAR OF FLYING SECTION 62.

"Douai, May 7th, 1916.
So far, little has happened in May. On the whole the weather has been good, but the English have no more desire to fly, for they come only very, very seldom. On April 25th a squadron of them got to Cambrai, but unfortunately escaped without damage. On May 5th our section finished its first year.

We made it the occasion of a little successful festivity in the mess. Our captain mentioned in a speech that the section had made about 1,000 war flights, with a total distance flown of over 94,000 kilometres. In the course of these flights we shot down 25 enemy machines, 20 of which fell into our hands. Our losses were two machines, which were captured by the English (on October 10th, 1915, and April 4th, 1916).

Do you know what section Franz has joined? I have not yet got a photo of myself with the Crown Prince of Saxony, but am trying to obtain one. I feel in very good health. I need the salve because my face is burnt (with the sun). The skin is peeling off. I have once more been eating to bursting point from the boxes. Further supplies will be very welcome. I have received the Easter eggs, chocolate hares and ginger-breads. For these also my heartiest thanks.

Monsieur Navarre's nine machines are a whopping lie. Five of them landed behind our lines. It is quite right to count those which crash in the enemy's lines, for the main thing is to put the machines and crews out of action.

One can hardly see any harm in the proceedings in the Reichstag as long as they are started by that fellow Liebknecht. The man must be dotty. These peace bleatings are superfluous; this is the time when we must put all our strength into the war.

THE FIFTEENTH

> Lieutenant Immelmann shot down his fifteenth enemy aircraft westward of Douai.
> *Excerpt from the official military communiqué of May 17th, 1916.*

"*Douai, May 18th, 1916.*
Many cordial thanks for your two last letters and the boxes.

This time I shall not answer your letters, but merely tell you some things. You will have read the telegram stating that I polished off No. 15. But you will perhaps ask: what about No. 14? No 14 is the one I shot down over Monchy on April 23 rd. I have already written you a short account of that.

I took off early on May 16th, but flew about for a long time without success. In the evening I wanted to test the climbing capacity of a new machine which a comrade had obtained a few days previously. In reality, I only meant to do a quick climb to 4,000 metres and then down again.

But when I was high up I saw they were firing at an aircraft somewhere in the front line. Then of course I had to go along and see what was up. I flew up and down at 4,200 metres; after a while I saw three biplanes far below me. One was about 2,800 metres up, and the other two perhaps 2,400. I could not make out the nationality markings on account of the thick haze. But as they were over German territory and no one was shooting at them, I thought they might be Germans. There was something funny about one of them, however. He seemed to be flying peaceably behind the other two, and yet he looked a different type. I decided to have a look at the fellow.

Down I go in a very steep dive, which brings me also horizontally nearer to him at a very great speed. When I have dropped down to 3,000 metres and am about 300–400 metres away from the three, I discover that the upper one is a Bristol biplane and the lower two L.V.G.s. The Englishman is pursuing one of the two Germans. As he is concentrating all his attention on him, he has not noticed me yet.

I dive still lower, and when I am within 30–40 metres of him and 10–20 above him, I get him in my sights and take careful aim. I fire both machine guns simultaneously—15–20 rounds from each. I must have hit him, for never have I been able to aim so calmly and deliberately.

The Englishman goes into a feeble right hand turn, which develops at once into a heel over by the right. Then, pushing his machine hard down, he flies a short distance westward, after which he promptly begins to spin—a sign that his fate is sealed. But he vanishes in the haze before he has finished his first spiral. So I cannot say whether he has crashed or not. If he is still alive, he will perhaps try to reach his lines. I therefore head for the front at once, so as to cut off his way back. But he does not appear. He must be down somewhere. So I fly home.

On reaching the aerodrome I report my fight and my supposition that the Englishman has probably crashed. Then I learn that a biplane of our section, which was pursued by an Englishman, shot the latter down near Izel. The biplane's observer says he was chased by an Englishman for quite a long time. He was somewhat late in recognising the latter's nationality, but when he did, he fired at him several times. Suddenly another Englishman—quite a small machine— appeared above him (this was really me) and fired, after which he vanished. Immediately afterwards the English biplane went down, and he fired at it during its fall.

After hearing this account I saw clearly that the Englishman must have been the one I attacked. We brought in the remains of the machine the following morning. It was a one-seater Bristol scout, equipped with a machine gun which could shoot forward and upward. The pilot was killed by a bullet through the body which passed into the cockpit from above and behind. There were other signs that proved hits from behind.

As the German biplane was ahead of the Englishman and below him, but I was behind and above him, it was evident that I must have fired the fatal shots. So to my great joy I am once more in the communiqué.

That's the right way to clasp the Order. Wait—it has just occurred to me that I have got two new Orders. One is the Iron Crescent, which is worn like the 1st Class Iron Cross, but on the right side. Then I have also got the 'Imbias' medal in silver, accompanied by a letter in the Turkish language.

You can see what the medal looks like from the photographs of Buddecke, who has just got the 'Pour le Mérite.'

I never fly an L.V.G. on duty, but only to instruct a comrade.

I still have the burnt carbine here.

Yesterday I received a card: 'God be with you! Maria Immaculata, Duchess of Saxony.' That's nice, isn't it?

The Duke of Altenburg was here yesterday; he knew Franz was a pupil on his aerodrome. I believe one of his sons was at the König Georg Grammar School with Franz. Franz wrote to me that he would like to get into our section. I am not at all for it. I wrote back to him that he must first make good as a war pilot.

I was also very pleased that my old bus E.13 was exhibited at the War Exhibition. It was quite right of you to give them one of my photographs in that case."

POPULARITY

"Many hearty thanks for your last letter. It gave me much fun.

So I am to always carry that leaf about with me. If I did the same with every lucky flower, every bit of clover, etc., I should carry a small kitchen garden with me. And then, for the sake of fairness, I should have to take along all the rosaries, crucifixes and other talismans which have been sent to me. There are, in fact, too many young girls with such bright ideas. I am sure they are all young ladies with very sensitive feelings. One thing is certain: their wishes are all well meant, and that is what gives me pleasure when I receive all these consignments.

Your letter of today is really humorous. I have had no further experiences."

In consequence of the days of bad weather extending from the end of May to the middle of June which followed the writing of this letter, it remained Max's last one to his mother. Apparently my brother considered the few activities in the air as little worthy of mention as the important changes which took place during the next few days and which opened a new path for him.

We obtain a picture of his last days from official reports and day-books and from accounts furnished by comrades and superiors.

SHOT DOWN BY HIS OWN GUN

On May 31st, a fine morning after the long period of bad weather seemed at last to promise a day of fruitful flying activities. My brother was on the aerodrome at an early hour with his Fokker pilots. During the usual 'coquetting with the machine,' as he liked to call it, a report came through that an enemy formation of seven machines had crossed the lines near Serre in the neighbouring sector and was heading towards Bapaume and Cambrai. My brother took off at once with Lieutenant Mulzer and Corporal Heinemann.

The fire of the anti-aircraft batteries indicated clearly the route taken by the enemy formation. Between Bapaume and Cambrai they climbed to the height at which the seven Vickers machines were flying. The latter bore off towards the front at once when the three Fokkers attacked them. In the course of their turn two Englishmen flying a bit lower were hustled away from their formation. One of them was attacked and subjected to a heavy fire by my brother; apparently it was hit, for it strove to reach the front in a steep glide, but when pursued by Mulzer it eventually landed on German territory near Inchy.

When my brother saw Mulzer take up the pursuit of the stricken foe, he turned back to attack the rest of the enemy formation. His first glance showed him young Heinemann making up for inexperience by vigour and attacking the other isolated Englishman at very close quarters but failing to notice two other Vickers diving on him from above. In his efforts to protect Heinemann and divert these two opponents to himself my brother opened a continuous fire from far too great a distance. Then his Fokker suddenly reared up with a terrible jerk, which was followed by a horrible shaking and jolting. His hands Performed the right actions instinctively—gas off—ignition out.

Weird tremors accompanied the final revolutions of the engine which went round very irregularly with the driving forces of its 14 cylinders and only half a propeller, until at last a violent jerk brought it to a standstill, and at the same moment the machine whirled down into the depths over its left wing.

What had happened? Was he hit—when still so far away from the enemy? Impossible! So once again a failure of the interruptor gear to function had caused the machine gun to shoot off a propeller blade!

A glance ahead, however, showed him the strange position of the remaining blade and admitted only one interpretation—the engine had slipped forward, and therefore the struts which held it in position must be broken! But from behind him a curious clicking, creaking sound made itself heard through the howl of the wind in the bracing wires. A backward glance—the rudder is flapping aimlessly in the wind—pressure on the rudder-bar tells its own tale, for his foot moves forward without encountering any resistance, as if pushing against a mass of cotton wool. Out of control? And now the ground shoots up towards him at an alarming speed!

He moves the stick with a cautious hand ... thank heaven, it encounters a certain amount of pressure—the elevator wires appear to be intact. Then ... in response to the control movement, the engine seems to have pulled itself up again slightly, for a strange jerk quivers through the machine. The pilot is prompt to assist this upward movement by pulling his stick a bit further—and another bit ... will the wings hold? ... the machine's nose comes up slowly, and at 500 metres off the ground the fearful fall is checked. Then he pushes the stick down again and again to prevent the engine slipping backward and causing another fall, but he can feel when it is necessary to pull the machine up again slightly so that his steep glide may not turn into a descent out of control. In this fashion he goes down towards the ground, and now the dreaded moment which is to show whether he can flatten out in time has come and gone. The machine and its exhausted pilot are safely down on the gentle slope of a meadow verging on the road which leads from Cambrai to Douai.

The results shown by an inspection of the engine are far from pleasing. The first fearful tremors produced a devastating effect when they hurled the irregularly revolving masses at the machine after the destruction of the propeller blade! Only two struts still hold the engine to the machine, and they are dangerously bent, while the bracing wires are entwined with the rudder control wires in a disorderly entanglement. A little more, and the wings would have collapsed like the sides of a house of cards, while the fuselage fell like a stone into the depths!

Deep as the shadows may have been which the impressions of that morning left on his mind, the welcome given by Germany's most popular pilot to the committee of 'neutral officers' who came to Douai specially to see him was cheerful and affable when he met them on his aerodrome a few hours later. Their visit called for particular friendliness, because they were the representatives of the few remaining nations that had not joined in the general battue organised against Germany.

There were two representatives of Nordic lands in the persons of a Swiss and a Dutchman; a Spaniard was there from the small neutral western corner of Europe, while an Argentinian stood for America and a Chinese for Asia. There was not much real neutrality left anywhere else in the world.

That same evening the section held another unpretentious celebration of a victory. The foeman shot down that morning was not credited to my brother, but to Lieutenant Mulzer, since the latter had barred the Vickers sent down by Immelmann from a possible way of escape across the lines. This victory was a noteworthy one, because it meant that Mulzer would be cited in the official communiqué for having brought down his fourth victim.

THE BEGINNINGS OF FORMATION FLYING

A succession of rainy days allowed the Fokker formation only brief patrols on June 4th and 8th. At last the weather improved towards midday of the 17th, on which day my brother took off twice with his Fokker pilots when reports came in from neighbouring sectors that enemy aircraft had crossed the lines. In neither case did it come to a fight, because the enemy machines sheered away from the sector of the 6th Army and flew back to their own territory.

Although those June days had brought so far but few flying activities, they were nevertheless important for my brother himself and also for the further development of the German air arm. Almost every day he met Major Stempel, the Aviation Staff Officer of the 6th Army, with whom he discussed the organisatory and general problems of aviation. Major Stempel writes as follows:

"He visited me almost every evening to report the experiences of his many airfights. Together we formulated the deductions to be drawn from them by the other fighting pilots of the 6th Army, and these we issued to them in the form of advice and definite instructions. By means of his simple diagrams he inspired us with such faith in the efficacy of his methods of attack that they were soon allowed to become common property of all the fighting pilots of the 6th Army...."

In the course of these discussions my brother pressed continually for a better grouping of the one-seater pilots. From Major Stempel, who had proved his worth as organiser of the pre-war Bavarian aviation corps, he found complete sympathy for his ideas, but very powerful opposition had to be broken down before the scheme could be carried out. At last, on June 10th, the first step was taken when the one-seater fighter Staffels were placed under the direct command of the Army H.Q. The chief consequence of this was that the one-seater fighters were at least under the sole command of the Aviation Staff Officer of the 6th Army (Major Stempel), so that it was at last possible to employ all of them in a methodical manner.

Although my brother did not live to see this organisation scheme, of which he was the co-originator, adopted by the other armies on account of its success and its final extension, by virtue of which all the aviation units attached to any army were subordinated to the authority of that army's O.C. Aviation (a post which was created later), he nevertheless experienced another great pleasure!

He was the first pilot to receive instructions to raise his own one-seater Staffel. Yet a bitter drop of wormwood was mingled with the joy and pride he felt at being chosen as the leader of the first German Jagdstaffel, for it meant separation from his dear old Flying Section 62 and its leader, Captain Kastner!

It was not merely separation but parting, for June 13th brought marching orders to the section, which was transferred to the Eastern Front, and the promotion of Captain Kastner to the command of a fighting squadron.

A PREMONITORY FAREWELL

So now at last the natural course of developments and promotions brought the hour of farewell! It is strange that my brother survived the departure of his old section by only three days! It was the section with which he had left Döberitz for the front on May 13th, 1915, to which he had belonged until June 13th, 1916, i.e., for an unbroken period of thirteen months, in which he gathered all his war experiences and won triumphs that were unparalleled for so young a pilot!

The parting from his old section-leader was a particularly painful one, for Captain Kastner, who was inspired by the true spirit of aviation, was the man who recognised his flying ability so soon, promoted his development in every direction and smoothed his upward path to fame and success.

Was it this parting—was it a premonition that made him so thoughtful during his last few days? However, the formation of 'his' Jagdstaffel promptly absorbed all his energies. Lieutenant Moosmeier, the leader of the Bavarian Flying Section 5b, which came to Douai to replace Flying Section 62 and shared a mess with my brother and his Fokker pilots, stated that although he was very silent and thoughtful in those days, he spoke with much pleasure of the formation of 'his' Jagdstaffel and the task of initiating younger comrades into the craft of scout-flying.

He likewise spoke hopefully of the new biplane scout which he was to be the first of the fighting pilots to receive some time within the next few days, for on the English side of the lines new fast one-seaters had made their appearance and proved themselves superior in climbing capacity to the Fokker.

But Destiny did not permit him to be unfaithful to the Fokker. Not until the day on which Douai said farewell to her dead protector did his new Halberstadt reach the aerodrome, and it was not he but his old war comrade Boelcke who flew this new biplane scout at the front for the first time.

THE FIRST COMBATS ON THE LAST DAY

The dawn of June the 18th brought clouds which descended lower and lower, but towards noon the sky cleared and the sun forced a way through, scattering the last shreds of cloud before it.

But it was not until 5 p.m. that enemy aircraft were first reported in sight. A formation of 8 English machines, proceeding from the direction of Arras, had the obvious intention of paying a visit to the territory of the 6th Army. My brother and three other Fokker pilots took off to give them a worthy reception.

When this formation discovered the Fokkers on its way to St. Quentin, it made for the lines again. My brother succeeded in bringing it to bay before it reached the front. In the dog-fight which followed the English machines tried to keep the Fokkers off their necks by tactics of mutual protection and so reach the salvation of the lines. My brother was the only pilot who succeeded in forcing one of these enemy aircraft down in a steep glide after a hard fight, and according to information subsequently received from the anti-balloon battery of Grévillers this Englishman landed near Bucquoy.

But while the now distant Englishmen dive down into the ground haze as seven black smudges, the four Fokkers fly up and down the front in good order and at a great height. Then, seeing that no further foreign birds disturb the peace of this sector, they make for their home aerodrome. One after the other, they dive down and are lost to view in the violet swathes of mist looming over the ground. But the lonely 'Eagle of Lille' still flies his solitary circles, as though no longer able to leave the radiant blue of the sun-bathed heights. In the far distance cotton-wool balls of cloudlets from the German Archies rising up above the milk-white shimmer of the sun justify him in making another inspection of the front. Three Vickers machines are jogging along comfortably over La Bassée, and the last shells sprayed up to them hasten their undoubtedly wise intention to withdraw.

So now it is time to take farewell of the heights and the radiant sun, for after a two hours' flight there cannot be much petrol left! The ground is screwed up to the machine in a series of clean spirals, and then with a little hop the Fokker joins the five other comradely machines which stand in a faultless line.

Then follows the criticism which is the usual procedure after a day of flying. When it is finished all the pilots who are not down for Lieutenant Mulzer's late patrol go off homeward.

THE LAST FLIGHT AND THE LAST VICTORY

But they have been only a short time at table with the jovial Bavarians when a report comes in that seven Englishmen are crossing the lines near Sallaumines. It is followed by another, which states that Lieutenants Mulzer and Osterreicher are involved in a severe fight against odds.

The car is soon ready, and my brother and little Heinemann reach the aerodrome just as the third Fokker of the patrol is climbing skyward. But the 160 h.p. Fokker is not serviceable; in the course of the afternoon's fight several of its struts have been badly shot about and the wings have been ripped; the repairs are not yet finished. A hesitating glance meets Heinemann's eye—no, let him fly his 160 h.p. machine himself, for the 100 h.p. reserve machine will do its duty!

Heinemann takes off. Brother Max is the last to go up, Shortly after 9.30 p.m. The Archies can be plainly seen to be firing like mad things over Lens, so that is the direction to take.

He reaches the 2,000 metres over Loos, turns back to the front and then towards Douai. Before him, but about 500 metres above his head, he sees the seven Englishmen and his four Fokkers. Away to north-eastward two Fokkers are engaged with four Englishmen, while somewhere above Henin-Liétard the other couple are getting into position to attack the other group of three Englishmen. But the German anti-aircraft guns are still blazing away at this last group of five machines, apparently on the assumption that the Fokkers have not yet climbed to the enemy's height.

When he approaches the group, which is now engaged in a battle of turns, he fires a white signal light, which is the well-known sign to the artillery that they must cease fire because they are endangering German machines. Then he climbs above the enemy in a wide turn and dives on to one of the Englishmen.

Continuous fire from both barrels induces the Vickers to make for the front in a steep dive. Meanwhile two machines detach themselves from the north-eastern group; one is a Vickers which hopes to relieve the comrade by diving on to the German who is renewing his attack and the other a Fokker (Lieutenant Mulzer). Then two other Fokker pilots (Sergeant Prehn and Corporal Heinemann) believing their dour Staffel-leader to be in danger from the diving Vickers, draw off from their opponents. Prehn succeeds in engaging the new foeman, leaving his Staffel-leader free to deal with his original opponent.

But at this moment Heinemann cruises unmolested over the scene, and his eyes take in the following events:

While Prehn is exchanging shots with the new Vickers, the Staffel-leader closes up with his Englishman, who heels over and falls headlong a few seconds later. Heinemann sees

Immelmann follow the enemy down in his steep glide, and now another Fokker hurtles past Immelmann and pursues the Vickers to the depths. It is Lieutenant Mulzer, whom lack of petrol has compelled to land, and so he accompanies the Vickers earthward to prevent the possibility of an escape across the lines.

The Englishman puts his Vickers down smoothly on a meadow close to Lens. My brother has taken good aim at his last victim, as the numerous hits on the machine testify. The pilot has been wounded in the shoulder, and considerable loss of blood has induced him to make the speediest possible landing.

But Heinemann then notices that his Staffel-leader has seen the escort follow his victim and so turns to the other Englishmen, utilising the 1,000 metres separating him from the nearest of them to climb a bit. Then Immelmann's Fokker suddenly rears up, goes down over the left wing, attains a level position again and flies ahead with strange lashing movements of its tail.

Now Heinemann must turn his attention to the enemy once more, for three Vickers machines are diving on Prehn, who is still engaged with his opponent. And so he is not compelled to witness the end of his Staffel-leader.

Eye-witnesses from the ground report as follows:

After a series of oscillations, which were plainly visible from the ground, the rear part of the fuselage suddenly detached itself from the fore part. The cockpit hurtled into the depths with the pilot, falling like a stone and making a weird whistling sound, while the wings collapsed like the sides of a house of cards, and came away from the shattered machine. The fore part of the machine, containing the engine and pilot, finished its fall of 2,000 metres with a dull thud.

Men opened the leather jacket of the dead pilot. They found the 'Pour le Mérite' ... and on the linen the monogram 'M.I.' ... Immelmann!

THE END

The two parts of the machine were found several hundred metres apart. Since the broken pieces of fuselage struts showed clean fractures, as if they had been cut apart, and since the machine had been seen by witnesses on the ground to break up in the air, the news went round quickly: 'Our Immelmann was shot down by a direct hit from an anti-aircraft gun!'

Several days later a commission composed of section-leaders of the 6th Army examined the debris and confirmed the opinion which the Fokker pilots had already formed.

While executing an almost horizontal glide with his engine throttled down nearly to half, Immelmann watched the steep glide of the Vickers he had wounded. When another Fokker hurtled after it into the depths, he made for an opponent who was still some distances away, meanwhile opening out to full revolutions the engine he had throttled down.

Then the Fokker suddenly reared up. With lightning speed the pilot switched off his engine. Once again, as on May 31st, he had shot off his own propeller! Once again the struts attached to the engine broke, once again the forward lurch of the engine plunged the machine into a fall. Once, and several times, he managed to pull the machine out of its uncontrolled descent.

But the light construction of the Fokker E. III could not

stand the strain of these repeated heavy blows. All its laboured upward movements were accompanied by weird creaking sounds in the hinder part of the machine, while some strange force, operating by a series of jerks, endeavoured to roll the machine over to the right.

It was well for the pilot that his work with the oscillating engine allowed him no time for a backward glance. Behind him two of the four longerons were already projecting into the air through the torn bracings, while every time he pulled the machine up, the tail part lashed upwards. Then the other two longerons broke, and with a mighty jerk the tail portion wrenched itself away from the control wires which still held it, and the steering surfaces folded up.

But the sounds of cracking and bursting all around him scarcely allowed the pilot to realise what was happening. Downward he plunged in his headlong fall; as the lights of Lille sparkled upwards to him, interspersed amid the dark shadows which the departing day cast on the ground, and before Mother Earth could take him to her arms, the counterpressure of the ground veiled his senses with merciful oblivion.

Perhaps, like a drowning man, he saw the events of his rich life flit past him as in a dream, or perhaps he sent a last greeting to his mother. Perhaps his joy of the fair summer's day that arrived at last after such a long bad spell and the beauteous flights in the radiant sunlight of the azure-blue sky came to him like the last pleasant thoughts of one who is about to fall asleep, or perhaps the proud elation of having brought his total up to seventeen by the victories of the afternoon and evening flitted through his senses. Then a deep, dreamless sleep overcame him, so that the sleeper knew not how hard was the bed on French soil on which he lay at rest.

Afterthoughts

No matter how much death-scorning daring was required of the individual achievements performed by the tenacious courage of our men in field-grey almost every day, scarcely a word of them reached the homeland from the massed battles of the world war, from the harrassing petty warfare of fronts petrified into trenches or from the holes in the earth that lay under a continuous hail of lead.

Was it then a wonder that the German nation listened attentively when names were mentioned for the first time in the impersonal official communiqué? They were the names of men to whom it was still permitted to conquer their foes in honourable knightly combats, as in the days of old. Was it a wonder that our two first fighting pilots, Boelcke and Immelmann, who added victory to victory in their sectors of the front and were mentioned again and again in the official communiqués, soon became true heroes of the people?

Then suddenly—and at first deemed but one of many rumours—came the news: 'Our Immelmann, the Eagle of Lille, is no more!'

The official communiqué which named his name for the last time put an end to all doubts, and the entire German nation mourned for its own hero-pilot in deepest sympathy!

Countless were the manifestations of sympathy which came from all classes of the German nation and its allied powers. They came from the Emperor and the King of Saxony, as well as from the most humble individuals. Only one who has seen the hundreds of telegrams, letters and poems which poured in daily for a period of many weeks can measure the depth to which this love for its fighting pilot penetrated the hearts of the German nation.

But the enemy also showed in chivalrous fashion his sympathy at the heroic death of his dreaded opponent who compelled the greatest respect from him in his lifetime. It sounds scarcely credible that in a world war waged by millions on either side the name of one individual should be so familiar to the enemy as it was clearly shown to be by a memorandum issued by the Chief of War Aviation in November, 1915, wherein it is stated that: "in a note dropped behind the German lines Lieutenant Immelmann was challenged to an aerial duel under defined conditions by an English officer-pilot". It is therefore easy to understand that wreaths in honour of the 'Gallant and Chivalrous Opponent' were dropped behind the German lines by representatives of the Royal Flying Corps and various British squadrons as soon as his death became known on their own side. One of these English machines flew down over Velu aerodrome, where Flying Section 32 were stationed, to a height of 50 metres. As any flight performed at only a few hundred metres so deep in our hinterland was attended by the greatest danger to life, this was something more than a chivalrous gesture.

I went to the scene of my brother's activities and triumphs in order to bring him home. Lieutenant Mulzer, his most successful pupil and the next after him to earn the 'Pour le Mérite', received me with an air of thoughtful melancholy and showed me round. His careful, calm, self-composed nature reminded me so very much of Brother Max.

His letters and photographs had made everything so familiar to me. There was his 160 h.p. Fokker, which he did not use on his last flight; there were the aerodrome, mess, comrades and superiors!

Love, honour, appreciation and mourning streamed out towards me, giving proof of the gap his death had made. The little group of Fokker pilots he led was deeply stricken, but none of them were destined to see the first anniversary of their master's death.

There was a foreboding in the condolence expressed by Boelcke, who had flown over from the Verdun sector to take leave of his old comrade of aerial warfare: "An accident—he shot his own propeller off! He was unconquered! Well for him that he found such a swift and beautiful soldier's death!"

At the fifth hour of June 22nd the 6th Army and the Front said farewell to him.

The coffin lay in state in the garden of the hospital in Douai, in the centre of a grove of laurels and cypresses, where it was surrounded by wreaths and covered with a sea of roses. It was flanked by four pillars, crowned with iron braziers, from which glowing flames rose up to heaven. The men who had formerly tended his Fokker furnished the guard of honour; before them there stood an immense crowd of field-grey warriors. It included Crown Prince Rupprecht of Bavaria, who commanded the army to which he was attached, Prince Ernst Heinrich, the son of the King of Saxony, all the generals holding commands in the 6th Army, the Chief of War Aviation and deputations from all the aviation units of the Western Front.

When the Aviation Staff Officer paid honour to him as a man and a soldier on behalf of the aviation corps, his final words were spoken to the accompaniment of the music which the dead man had loved so dearly. It was the song of the engines that descended from his Fokker pilots in the air above him.

A last greeting came from his faithful followers, for when the coffin reached the station and was being lifted from the gun-carriage into the van which was to convey it home, bounteous streams of roses poured down upon it from the air.

Three volleys resounded over the van, and while the melancholy strains of the ballad of the good comrade rose up, the army took leave of the airman who had kept faithful watch over Lille so often.

And now he returned home to Dresden. Thousands awaited him in silent mourning, thousands lined the streets, thousands accompanied the dead airman on his last journey from the station to the Tolkewitz cemetery.

How bravely mother bore the parting! "We will not mourn," she said. "See how all their thoughts are on him, and in these thoughts he will live on!" The further consequences of this resolution: "We will put on no signs of outward mourning" met with great response in Germany at that time, and Cæsar Flaischlen did honour to this unselfish attitude in a poem which he dedicated to my mother in memory of my brother's death.

It was a hero's funeral that Dresden gave her well-beloved son in the grove of urns in Tolkewitz. It was touching to see how tens of thousands took their leave of him, how tens of thousands stood closely thronged in reverential silence under the glowing sun of that June 25th while the funeral ceremonies took place in the Memorial Hall, where representatives of the Highest War Lord and the King of Saxony, the Saxon officers of highest rank, interminable deputations of aviation units, students' associations, and the authorities and representatives of his native town paid the last honours to the dead man.

But once again the engines of a Staffel sang high above, while a Zeppelin soared majestically a few metres over the tree tops of the grove of urns. From its gondola roses were dropped as a last farewell greeting from the members of the air corps who were on home service.

Then, while the triumphant song of the propellers said its farewell and died away in the distance and while the flames united over the remains of a dead German airman the song of all Germans resounded outside the Memorial Hall

Deutschland, Deutschland über alles!

Twelve years passed over the land. The tumult of the November Revolution and the penury of the inflation period swept through Germany. But these events could not stop the ex-airmen, students and all who did not forget 'their Immelmann' from raising stone upon stone. At last the statue created by Professor Pöppelmann was to be unveiled.

Our mother was almost seventy years of age when she flew from Zürich—where she now lives with her daughter, sad at heart because so far from her native land—to Dresden in order to attend the dedication of the memorial to her son in the Tolkewitz grove of urns. It was the first time in her life that she experienced the beauty of flight.

All were assembled there who had ties with him or with aviation. Major Rosenmüller, of the German Air Travel League, recalled memories of the true comrade to all, of the teacher of those who came after him and of the warrior whose chivalry was recognised by the foemen that first named him the 'Eagle of Lille'.

His statue and his name, said the speaker, should be an exhortation to us who were witnesses of Germany's collapse to hold our heads high and an exhortation to the younger generation to emulate the deeds of their predecessors. As this exhortation to the younger generation was uttered, the coverings fell and revealed in all its simple beauty the figure of a youth with uplifted face and one arm stretched upward to the sun, symbolic in its attitude of Max Immelmann's constant triumphant flights to the realms of light.

Then, to the strains of the Airmen's March, wreath after wreath is laid at the foot of the statue.

Once again—as on that day twelve years before—the song of all Germans rises up. It brings no message of hope to our ears; it only wakens memories of all the sacrifices which were apparently so useless, and we return without hope to the grey of everyday life.

When Captain Leeson laid a wreath at the feet of his former conqueror, the Eagle of Lille, in 1932, it showed us that his name was not forgotten abroad.

But his name must also live on in our younger generation, which is turning again with enthusiasm to the flying which he loved above everything. His essentially German nature in combination with his will—steeled to the utmost—to give everything for his country, his modesty and his complete subordination of his own personality can and must be an example to our youth.

May his statue of honour in the grove of urns in Dresden therefore prove an exhortation to young Germany to keep in memory the name of our first fighting airman and the pioneer of Germany's honourable place in the air.

Appendix

THE VICTORIES OF MAX IMMELMANN

VICTORY	DATE	TYPE	SERIAL	SQDN	TIME	CREW	FATE
1	1 Aug 1915	BE2c	—	2	1615 A	Lt. W. Reid	WIA/POW
2	26 Aug	Scout			pm		Killed?
3	21 Sep	BE2c	—	10	1000	2/Lt. S. W. Caws Lt. W. H. Sugden-Wilson.	Killed? WIA/POW
4	10 Oct	BE2c	2003	16	1500	2/Lt. J. Gay Lt. D. Leeson	WIA/POW WIA/POW
5	26 Oct	VFB5	5462	11	0955	Capt. C. C. Darley 2/Lt. R. L. Slade	WIA/POW POW
6	7 Nov	BE2c	1715	10	1445 B	Lt. O. V. LeBas Capt. T. D. Adams	Killed? Killed?
7	15 Dec	Morane	5087	3	am	Lt. A. V. Hobbs Lt. C. E. G. Tudor-Jones	Killed? Killed?
8	12 Jan 1916	VFB5	5460	11	0900 A	2/Lt. H. T. Kemp 2/Lt. S. Hathaway	WIA/POW Killed?
9	2 Mar	Morane	5137	3	am	Lt. C. W. Palmer Lt. H. F. Birdwood	DOW Killed?
10	13 Mar	Bristol	4678	4	1355 B	Maj. V. A. B-Kennett	Killed?
11	13 Mar	BE2c	4197	8	1740	Lt. G. D. L. Grune 2/Lt. B. E. Glover	Killed? Killed?
12	29 Mar	FE2b	6352	23	1100	2/Lt. F. G. Pinder 2/Lt. E. A. Halford	WIA/POW POW
13	30 Mar	BE2c	4116	15	1100 B	2/Lt. G. J. L. Welsford Lt. W. Joyce	Killed? POW
14	23 Apr	VFB5	5079	11	am	2/Lt. W. C. M. Phelan 2/Lt. W. A. Scott-Brown	POW POW
15	16 May	Bristol	5301	11	1800 A	2/Lt. M. M. Mowat	Killed?
16	18 Jun	FE2b	6940	25	1700	Lt. C. S. Rogers 3613 Sgt. H. Taylor	Killed? WIA/POW
17	18 Jun	FE2b	4909	25	2145 A	Lt. L. B. Savage 103872 A. M. Robinson	Killed? WIA/POW

NOTES

Victory No. 1
> Second Lieutenant William Reid, RFC, Royal Aero Cert. No. 1128 dated 16 March 1915.

Victory No. 2
> Was probably a French single seater machine.

Victory No. 3
> Second Lieutenant Stanley Winther Caws from the Isle of Wight. Former trooper with Paget's Horse in South Africa. In Canada when war started, he joined the 1st Canadian Contingent and transferred to the RFC in February 1915. Aero Cert. No. 1097 dated 25 February 1915. William Hodgson Sugden Wilson, West Somerset Yeomanry TF/RFC; Aero Cert. No. 1218 dated 22 April 1915.

Victory No. 4
> Second Lieutenant John Gay RFC (SR) Aero Cert. No. 1135 dated 30 March 1915.

Victory No. 5
> Captain Charles Curtis Darley, Royal Artillery/RFC, Aero Cert. No. 592, 15 August 1913. Escaped and commanded 88 Sqdn. in 1918. Later Group Captain CBE AM RAF.
> Second Lieutenant Slade seconded to RFC from Cyclist Corps.

Victory No. 6

> Lieutenant Owen Vincent LeBas, 1st Queen's Royal West Surrey Regt/RFC. Aero Cert. No. 1252, 29th April 1915. Wounded with West Surrey's, October 1914. Transferred to RFC as Observer in early 1915. Aged 21, educated at Charterhouse.
>
> Captain Adams, 1st West Lancs Brig RFA/RFC, aged 26.

Victory No. 7

> 2/Lt. Alan Victor Hobbs 10th Royal Sussex Regt/RFC, Aero Cert. No. 11552 April 1915. To France July. Reading Maths at Cambridge in 1914; aged 21. He was flying a Morane Parasol.
>
> 2/Lt. Tudor-Jones East Lancs Regt./RFC.

Victory No. 8

> 2/Lt. Herbert Thomas Kemp, Cheshire Regt./RFC; Aero Cert. No. 1231, 11 May 1915.

Victory No. 9

> Lt. Charles Walter Palmer, 9th Battn Leicestershire Regt./RFC; Aero Cert. No. 1497, 24 July 1915. Suffered blood poisoning on having a foot amputated and died 29 March 1916. He was flying a Morane Biplane.
>
> Lt. Herbert Frederick Birdwood, 20th London Regt., attached RFC. Educated Peterhouse, Cambridge. Nephew of Sir George Birdwood. Fought at Battle of Loos March 1915. Aged 22.

Victory No. 10

Major Victor Annesley Barrington-Kennett, Royal Engineers/RFC. Aero Cert. No. 190, 5 March 1912. Third of four sons of Lt. Col. B-K, of the King's Bodyguard to die in WW1. He was flying a single seat Bristol Scout, and had been mentioned in Despatches. He received his education at Eton and Balliol College, Oxford.

Victory No. 11

Lieutenant Gilbert Dennis James Grune, RFA/RFC. Fought in France before transferring to the RFC. Aero Cert. No. 1387, 3 July, 1915. Returned to France in November.

Victory No. 12

Second Lieutenant Frank George Pinder RFC; Aero Cert. No. 1825, 2 October 1915.
Second Lieutenant E. A. Halford, Wiltshire Regt. and RFC.

Victory No. 13

Second Lieutenant George Joseph Lightbourn Welsford, Middx Regt./RFC. To France from Sandhurst, wounded 9 May 1915. Learned to fly (Aero Cert. No. 1702, 6 September, 1915), joined RFC, returning to France in February 1916. Aged 20, he was educated at Harrow, Marlborough and Caius, Cambridge. Lieutenant Wayland Joyce had been at school with Welsford, and been commissioned in the Bedford Regt.

Victory No. 14

> Second Lieutenant Phelan, RFC Special Reserve.
> Second Lieutenant W. A. Scott-Brown, Argyle and Sutherland Highlanders attached to RFC.

Victory No. 15

> Second Lieutenant Morden Maxwell Mowat RFC; Aero Cert. No. 2064, 11 November 1915.

Victory No. 17

> Lieutenant John Raymond Boscawen Savage RFC, aged 17 and educated at Oundle College. Aero Cert. No. 1913, 18 October, 1915. Son of Major A. R. B. Savage RFA, grandson of Colonel H. J. Savage 91st Highlanders, who fought in Boer War, great grandson of General Sir John Savage KCB who commanded the Marines in the Battle of the Nile.

GLOSSARY

A	Approximately
B	British time (all others are German)
DOW	Died of Wounds
WIA	Wounded in Action
POW	Prisoner of War

Norman L. Franks 1990